APP
VANISH

Stealth Concepts for Effective Camouflage and Concealment

Matthew Dermody

APPEAR TO
VANISH

Stealth Concepts for Effective Camouflage and Concealment

Matthew Dermody

Front cover photo credit: Shawn Swanson

Back cover photo credit: Adam Grimm

The A-TACS AU camouflage pattern is a registered trademark of Digital Concealment Systems, LLC and used with permission.

Visit the author's website at www.hiddensuccesstactical.com

Like Hidden Success Tactical on Facebook and follow the author on Twitter @AppearToVanish

Dermody, Matthew

Appear to vanish: stealth concepts for effective camouflage and concealment/ Matthew Dermody -- 3rd Ed.

ISBN: 978-1-7266-1172-5

1. Camouflage. 2. Concealment. 3. Surveillance. 4. Stealth 5. Hunting I. Title

Third Edition

Printed in the United States of America

10 9 8 7 6 5 4 3 2

Other published works by Matthew Dermody:

Books:

GRAY MAN: Camouflage for Crowds, Cities, and Civil Crisis

Hidden Success: A Comprehensive Guide to Ghillie Suit Construction

Website Resources: (www.hiddensuccesstactical.com)

Civilian and Military Camouflage Patterns - General Editor (free download)

Inexpensive Winter Ghillie Blanket

3 Reasons to Stock Up on Halloween Make-Up

The Tactical Drawbacks of High-Definition (HD) Camouflage Patterns

Guest Blogs:

Six Materials for Field Expedient Natural Camouflage - @www.WillowHavenOutdoor.com

Do You Really Need A Ghillie Suit? - @www.itstactical.com

Build Your Own Ghillie Suit for Under $75 - @www.itstactical.com

Practical Alternatives for Buried Survival Caches - @www.survivalschool.us

Acknowledgements

A special thank you goes out to David Scott-Donelan, for his photos, insights, and the counsel and encouragement to pursue a traditional publishing route over self-publishing.

Thank you to Philip Duke of Digital Concealment Systems, LLC for granting permission to feature the A-TACS AU camouflage pattern on the book cover. A-TACS AU is a registered trademark of Digital Concealment Systems, LLC and used with permission.

Much appreciation is due wildlife artist, Adam Grimm (of Million Dollar Duck fame and two-time Federal Duck Stamp Competition winner) for his back cover photo and great enthusiasm for my writing projects. His artwork can be viewed and purchased at www.adamgrimm.com.

To my friend, Shawn Swanson, a true modern day warrior, who field-tested my ghillie suits along the Arizona-Mexico border with great success. The concepts of effective camouflage and concealment culminated in the excellent photos he provided for the book and front cover.

To Stephanie Hoffman, for granting me permission to use her wonderful five senses graphics. You may view more of her work at www.stephhoffman.com

And, finally, endless thanks to my lovely wife and my beautiful twin daughters for their continued support and encouragement in my writing endeavors.

Legal Disclaimer

Reviews:

"There are very few books and videos available today on what I would call "sustainable concealment". To merely put on a camouflaged pattern uniform and neglect the rest of the requirements is neither "camouflage" nor "concealment". Matt Dermody's book thoroughly covers all the necessary points on how to appear to vanish. As a professional soldier, I heartily recommend this book and believe that it will fill a niche that is currently open and needs to be filled.

- **David Scott-Donelan**, author of *Tactical Tracking Operations: The Essential Guide for Military and Police Trackers* and CEO and founder of the Scott-Donelan Tracking School

"Another great job by Matt Dermody. This thorough study of human stealth and camouflage lives up to its title, and forces you to "think" camouflage in all its subtleties."

- **Major John L. Plaster**, US Army Special Forces (Ret.) and author of *Ultimate Sniper* books and videos

"Appear to Vanish gives a unique and introspective look into what every tactical operator knows intellectually but does not necessarily apply pragmatically...a resource guide that nails it on every page."

- **Ty Cunningham**, Retired U.S. Marshal, and Tactical Commander, U.S. Marshals Scout-Tracker Units (District of Alaska and Wyoming)

"Matt Dermody has stepped into the realm of the masters when it comes to the functionality and the use of camouflage. I haven't seen anyone since the combat trackers of Vietnam who understands more about the art and science of camouflage. This book should become a standard manual for military and law enforcement throughout the world and is a must read for anyone who wants to understand the true meaning of the proper use of camouflage in any environment."

- **David Everheart**, Certified Senior Scout tracker and GTSB Lead Examiner (Eastern United States)

Table of Contents

"The unseen enemy is always the most fearsome."

- **George R.R. Martin**, *A Clash of Kings*

The Need for Camouflage

Effective camouflage influences and enhances the mission success of *sniping, scouting and surveillance, survival*, and *strategy sports*.

I am obsessed with all things camouflage. There is something about putting on camouflage clothes or a ghillie suit and slipping out into nature undetected with the sole purpose of staying undetected. Whether from man or beast, camouflage and concealment is deeply rooted in the fundamentals of survival. Ever since adolescence, I remember the fun of playing war and hide-n-seek in the backyard with siblings and friends. To this day, I often go out along nature trails and simply sit, concealed in camouflage and observe the people who casually and unknowingly pass me by. This is the motivation behind *Appear to Vanish.* Whether for professional or recreational reasons, the concepts discussed within will broaden your knowledge on how to conceal yourself properly and effectively.

So, to begin, *what* is camouflage? Webster's Dictionary defines camouflage as "the disguising of troops, ships, guns, etc. to conceal them from the enemy, as by the use of paint, nets, or leaves in patterns merging with the background."[1] Another good working definition is "the use of natural and artificial material on personnel, objects, structures, or tactical positions for the purpose of intentionally confusing, misleading, or evading an enemy force."[2] My own simplest, two-word definition of camouflage is "transparent presence".

It is also important to define and explain the difference between cover and concealment. Cover provides a person shelter from the elements or from incoming fire near their position, reducing an enemies' ability to put "rounds on target". Concealment, on the other hand, provides protection from observation and detection.

This moth is a perfect example of passive mimetic camouflage. Photo by David Scott-Donelan

Camouflage is the active or passive expression of crypsis, a method in which something or someone remains indiscernible from the surrounding environment by means of deception, concealment, and mimicry. Camouflage does not make the wearer invisible or undetectable. Its primary purpose, as mentioned earlier, is to create sensory confusion and thereby making it more difficult to discern the human shape, profile, and outline.

Camouflage falls into two broad types: mimetic and disruptive. Mimetic camouflage is camouflage that mimics the surroundings. Disruptive camouflage focuses on deliberately making the discernment of objects more difficult by altering its appearance and outline.[3]

Typically, we view camouflage by a basic definition that describes the obscuring patterns printed on military and hunting clothing. More specifically, it is the colorations and design patterns that appear on that clothing. After all, the very concept of clothing is a type of camouflage: it is used to conceal our nakedness and obscure or disguise the way everyone else views us. The less clothing, or more formfitting apparel that we wear, the more revealed or revealing we become to others. Likewise, the opposite is true. The more clothes we wear and the looser the fit, the more those who look upon us, whether with disdain or desire, are forced to search for and use more information and/or imagination to decipher our true form.

In life, we reveal more of our true selves to those with whom we have close relationships. The opposite holds true with our enemies. We attempt to keep them at greater distances, keep them guessing regarding our intentions and tactics, and keep secrets from them. That may seem extreme, but that is the reality for those in harm's way or those engaged in combat operations. Those who pursue stealth and concealment from a recreational aspect may not have the "life or death" urgency, but they still have a desire to remain undetected. We employ concealment tactics against two types of creatures: animals and other humans.

My previous book, *Hidden Success: A Comprehensive Guide to Ghillie Suit Construction*, dealt primarily with ghillie suit construction and all of its components. I briefly touched upon the topic of camouflage effectiveness to provide a basic overview. In the book, I merely referred to this subject as detection flags. Other resources, such as military field manuals refer to it as target indicators. If I were to adhere strictly to the "S" word concept, I would label these as signals. Whichever way you label them, they are discrepancies that can expose or disclose a hide location and foil the best attempts at concealment. The concepts listed in this book are the clues used by counter-snipers, trackers, Department of Natural Resources (DNR) game wardens, and surveillance teams to search for individuals trying to avoid detection. The point is that there are people trained on specific ways to detect others, even those hiding in camouflage clothing and ghillie suits.

The reason or reasons for detection avoidance are individually specific. As I am not an attorney or an expert in legal matters, know that you should carefully consider the legal ramifications and consequences of your pursuits. This book focuses on the practical application of fieldcraft techniques to eliminate or reduce these detection flags and that compliment the use of ghillie suits and other types of garment camouflage through the implementation and adherence to these stealth concepts. You may not be able to deceive the most highly trained individuals from detecting you, but with this book, you can make it much more difficult for the average person or animal to locate or detect you.

Throughout my research for this book and my previous work, I have found and read several books and manuals. I am a strong believer in teaching someone "how to fish" rather than just "giving them a fish". This creates and fosters the concept of self-reliance, which I find appealing. It may not be the best, consumer-dependent business model, but it is the right way to deal with people. That does not mean I teach pro bono, as I have no moral objection to making money to support my family. However, I do not sell products on my website that I am not also willing or prepared to teach or explain its proper use. With that approach in mind, I am usually available via email or by phone to help any customer or potential client with projects or problems.

I find there are always new things to learn, something new to address and something new to create. With that, our skill sets should continue on a forward trajectory. I have gone back to school as well--revisiting fieldcraft skills to make sure what I know is still relevant, retainable, and recallable--not just to teach the skills, but also to maintain my own level of proficiency. Although I teach others, I still consider myself a student who desires to learn more. My mantra is this: Whatever I learn, I pass on.

The basic concept of this book started from the desire to expound upon the five S's commonly found in numerous military field manuals regarding camouflage and concealment.[4]

The term visual saliency in the context of cognitive science describes the features that make objects detectable. Visual salience is the summary of certain factors that make humans stand out from their environment.[5]

These five S's are as follows:

- Shape
- Shadow
- Shine
- Silhouette
- Spacing
- Movement

You will immediately notice the addition of a non-S word to this list: *movement.* So many elements affect movement that the list creator(s) probably decided at the time it was much simpler to refer to it as movement. The word I use, *shifting*, most likely had some other relevant meaning or had the potential to confuse military personnel. Regardless, they chose not to use the word and I have because it fits into how I teach on the subject.

In my peculiar blend of thoroughness and overkill, I felt the need to go beyond the standard list of five and expand it. As with the prior list, each concept and its associated subcategories begin with the letter S to aid in memorization and to show the relation shared by each attribute. It may seem like a more mentally taxing to remember more S words, but they address some key concepts that are absent in other printed publications and field manuals.

There really is a science behind camouflage and concealment, but most readers of this book are not looking for bar graphs and research data. If you are like me, you want the principles that make camouflage and concealment possible, not a scientific journal or post-doctorate abstract on "how" camouflage and concealment work.

So what are the concepts for successful concealment? All of these concepts have an interesting relationship to one another because they are both interrelated and interdependent. No one concept alone will produce the necessary results. As one recognizes and incorporates the different concepts together, the success rate against detection grows exponentially. The concepts are as follows:

- Senses
- Spacing
- Shadow
- Shine
- Shifting
- Surface
- Surroundings
- Status Quo
- Study

In this book, I will explain the need to address each concealment concept and how it relates to the others. My goal is to provide you with the necessary information to take your fieldcraft concealment skills to their maximum potential and utilize the skills as an effective force multiplier.

Before I go any further, we must recognize the justifications for utilizing effective camouflage and concealment. These justifications are summarized in the successfulness of the following endeavors: sniping, scouting, surveillance, survival, and strategy sports (e.g., paintball and airsoft).

These concepts will help you decide what level of concealment you need for your particular application. In some instances, simple two-dimensional camouflage clothing may be all you need. In most scenarios, the addition of natural vegetation or a ghillie suit provides a much more effective camouflage and concealment protocol.

The selection of a starting camouflage pattern shows how several of the camouflage concepts are all interrelated and interdependent. For this reason, as you read the following factors that many people use to pick a camouflage pattern, specifically think about the concepts. These are the prime examples that predetermine the need to avoid focusing on one single concept when making camouflage and concealment decisions.

There are plenty of military and civilian camouflage patterns to choose from out there. Some are exceptionally good; some have the capability to be overwhelmingly bad. How good or how bad the patterns truly are depends on how you are planning to utilize them in your concealment scheme. Camouflage patterns alone do not make a great concealment doctrine, but debates over which camouflage pattern outperforms another are often found throughout Internet forums and social media pages. The debates are almost as bad as the infamous .45 ACP vs. 9mm arguments that seemed to appear in firearm magazine articles at least twice a year.

When it comes to camouflage patterns, like many people, I have my personal favorites and I do like some of the patterns that fall into the category of "eye candy". Most people, when they select a camouflage pattern, they typically do so based on some key factors that influence their decision making process. Let's discuss those factors.

1. **Latest pattern** - You must understand and realize an important factor in the camouflage business. New patterns are developed and created every couple of years in order for the manufacturers to remain relevant and to stay in business. The best camouflage developers know that to be successful, they must convince consumers that their concealment success directly relates to the purchase and use of a new camouflage pattern. Even the effective, proven patterns are not immune to further improvements in order to entice potential new customers or maintain previous ones. Oftentimes, you may discover your favorite pattern discontinued, simply because the demand had dropped, despite its success in your particular environment.

2. **Price** - Pure economics often comes into play in pattern selection, especially when the pattern is in high demand or is difficult to find. A sound budget and understanding of the camouflage concepts will save both your backside and your money. Beware of cheap imitation patterns produced in China.

3. **Endorsements** - Word of mouth is still the best form of advertising. The problem is you have to trust the mouth from which the accolade is coming. Here again, camouflage

developers hire marketing teams, celebrities, and recognized experts to help present their pattern as a legitimate choice for concealment.

4. **Country of origin** - As Americans, we are very proud of our country and despite current trends and statistics, we still think we are the best at everything. If you operate with the mentality that you will only wear American-made or US military-inspired camouflage patterns, you can overlook some of the most effective foreign military camouflage. While you may protest the lack of "Made in the U.S.A" patriotism involved in selecting foreign camouflage pattern(s), choosing such a pattern can give you a tactical edge--especially against a foe with limited knowledge of foreign camouflage who expects to find you wearing a pattern worn by your country's military forces or those commonly found in sporting goods stores.

5. **Pattern color** - The color palette consists of exact or similar colorations found within the environment you wish to conceal yourself. This is the biggest determining factor since the colors in the pattern must match or blend into the environment where the pattern is worn. An important thing to consider is the predominant color of most big game animals, upland birds, and small game animals. It is not green or any variant of green. Most are browns, tans, and grays with good reason. The various shades of browns, tans, and grays blend into more environments than any shade of green. So, if in doubt, choice brown dominant patterns, unless you can specifically justify the use of a green-dominant pattern.

6. **Availability** - This factor often limits your choice regarding certain camouflage patterns and the type of

garment you want or need. You may find exactly what you want, only to find out it is not available in your size or a particular garment style. Some patterns may be restricted or intended for strict military use. This forces you to search various retailers in order to find the clothing items you want and need. As the years go by, some patterns fade into obscurity because the demand for them has significantly decreased. Scavenging military surplus stores, garage and estate sales, or online auctions become the primary source for obtaining certain styles of clothing and patterns.

Base Layer Camouflage Pattern Importance

Whenever I teach classes on camouflage or consult with a client, I often use the following picture on page 13 to demonstrate the drawbacks of camouflage clothing, particularly on civilian hunting camouflage patterns. There are those who will argue that these, and similar patterns, will work in concealing the wearer from most animals. Others will argue that these types of camouflage patterns are unsuitable against the deductive and detective mind of the human adversary. However, with thoughtful additions, even high-definition camouflage patterns can have high potentials for effectiveness.

Visual Downfalls of HD Camouflage

- **Conflicting seasonal growth and dormancy** - Dead leaves and new growth do not appear in great amounts.

- **Different leaf/bark combination** - Check the camouflage pattern for leaves appearing to grow from or attached to limbs having bark from an incorrect/different tree species. Leaves that do not move in the wind exist only on printed objects and apparel.

- **Brand/logo/language detector** - Be aware of any obvious manufacturer logo or words on apparel. These markers also expose language/country of origin.

- **Different tree species occupying the same space** - This only happens rarely when seeds are distributed through animal droppings. Oftentimes, the foreign (or least predominant species will be relegated to a small sapling or will have a very noticeable maturity differential. The most noticeable mistake is the mix of coniferous and deciduous species.

- **Branch orientation** - Watch for conflicting branch orientation and unusual or unnatural directional growth.

- **Background color does not match the implied foreground hue and density** - The only times where the background will not match the foreground density is at clearings where heavily wooded areas open up into fields or meadows.

- **Wrong object size or proportions** - Certain objects within the pattern may be as much as twice their normal size in relation to those found in nature or on the pattern itself. I once found a Mossy Oak New Breakup-sublimated polyester T-shirt that had a several red oak leaves that were the size of giant sycamore leaves. I almost bought it strictly to serve as the proverbial bad example.

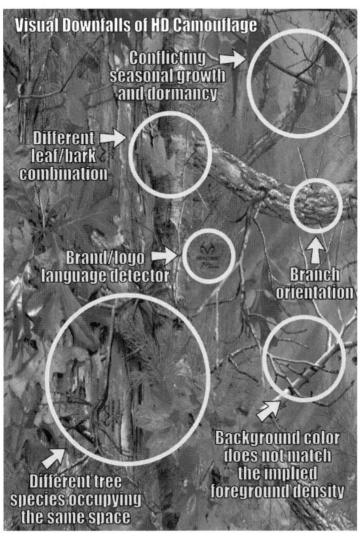

Visual Downfalls of HD Camouflage

Conflicting seasonal growth and dormancy

Different leaf/bark combination

Brand/logo language detector

Branch orientation

Different tree species occupying the same space

Background color does not match the implied foreground density

Visual downfalls of high-definition camouflage.

The photograph on the previous page displays some of the concepts and their lack of effectiveness. This is often a good starting point for understanding the differences between a pattern designed for static use and other patterns designed for mobile/kinetic use. Students and practitioners of camouflage and concealment can recognize proper camouflage discipline by analyzing different camouflage patterns. Careful study reveals advantages and disadvantages of each pattern studied. There are some exceptions, but generally speaking, there are no bad camouflage patterns, merely bad applications of them.

How to Apply Camouflaging Techniques

Applying camouflage--whether face paint, ghillie suits, or strictly all-natural camouflage--requires the following coloring and texturing techniques to be useful and effective. Eddie Starmater examines these techniques in *Principles of Natural Camouflage: The Art of Invisibility*, a great reference book dealing exclusively with natural camouflage as it relates to primitive survival skills. Starmater's book discusses the principles of camouflage from a strict, nature-only discipline, teaching others to use what is found in nature and in the surroundings to aid in camouflage and concealment. I highly recommend his book, as it has helped me to rely less upon commercially available camouflage and concealment products. His knowledge of positive and negative space and the principles of baseline alone, make his book a worthwhile read. He applies the following techniques to achieve amazing camouflage and concealment results:

- Background
- Blots
- Spots
- Stripes
- Highlights[6]

Another practitioner of natural camouflage is Creek Stewart, a wilderness survival instructor and owner of Willow Haven Outdoor (www.willowhavenoutdoor.com). He also is a well known for his work on The Weather Channel's TV shows, *Fat Guys in the Woods* and *SOS: How To Survive*. In the following photo, you can see how effective an application of mud and a covering of forest debris can change one's appearance.[7]

Survival expert, author and TV host, Creek Stewart, demonstrates the application of natural camouflage. Photo credit: Creek Stewart/www.willowhavenoutdoor.com

This is similar to the technique that was featured in the 2012 Lionsgate Film, *The Hunger Games*, based on the same novel by Suzanne Collins. While the Hollywood makeup and artwork were much more elaborate, the concepts of obscuring or eliminating the human outline were also present.

While I come from a different discipline regarding camouflage and despite some practitioners of natural camouflage choose to remove some articles of clothing, this is not necessary for natural camouflage effectiveness. Choosing neutral/drab gray or tan colored clothing as a base is a great start.[8] Because these colors blend well into many surroundings, it takes less time and materials to camouflage than normal street clothes, especially brightly colored ones. Later on in Chapter 5, the chapter addressing Shine, I will explain the use of camouflage face paint and its application.

Breaking up surface and shape issues from a strict, *natural* camouflage standpoint, using these S words:

- Sludge (mud and clay)
- Soil (dry dirt and dust)
- Scrub (sticks and stems)
- Stubble (loose grass and leaves)

The base layer of any natural camouflage scheme is going to include mud. Obtaining the right consistency is necessary in order for base layer of the mud to stay on the body or on clothing and provide proper adhesion of the loose soil, scrub, and stubble.

The four S's I use as application techniques for natural camouflage and face paint that produce the most effective results are:

- Striping
- Streaks
- Spots
- Splotches

The best way to break up surface and shape issues in your garment camouflage is to employ the three-dimensional aspects of natural vegetative and fabric camouflage with another subset of S's:

- Shrouds
- Scrim and scraps
- Scrub (sticks and stems)
- Sheaves and stubble

The base layer starts with the shroud, usually netting or a sniper veil. Added fabric scrim and scrap breaks up the outline and provides some texture. The scrub consists of the natural vegetative sticks, twigs, and woody stems from within the environment. Lastly, adding sheaves or bundled grasses, leaves, and other vegetative debris finishes the three-dimensional effect.

But why pay all this attention to camouflage and concealment in the first place? Do you really need all this head-to-toe concealment? The answer is an emphatic, "Yes!" It is as every bit as important as your weapon, your helmet, your reconnaissance gear, and tactics. If you do not plan for proper camouflage and concealment protocols, then you have failed to plan. Failing to plan can mean failing a hunt, failing a mission, or worse yet, failing to come home.

Senses

Effective camouflage disrupts or interferes with an adversary's senses of *sight, sound, and smell.*

In my last book, I discussed some of these camouflage concepts briefly as *detection flags*. These detection flags are inadamant objects that can visually expose or disclose a hide location and foil the best attempts at concealment. Some of these detectors do have a motion element and are more noticeable, but all can give away your position and your ability to achieve or maintain concealment. Determining whether you are avoiding detection from humans or from animals is important, in order to justify the employment of certain countermeasures. It is true that adopting certain concepts to avoid detection from animals will also aid in avoiding detection by humans.

Most often, we need to consider these stealth concepts when avoiding detection by humans. Human beings, as a whole, are the most intelligent species on the planet. It takes a deliberate, intentional effort to dupe another human. Because the human mind is capable of processing large amounts of audio and visual information, these identifiers raise mental flags, alerting a foe that something does not look right. However, just as people fall victim to financial schemes and other forms of trickery, the success or failure of a scheme or an attack has a direct correlation to the amount of knowledge held by the potential victim. The more knowledge one has regarding possible schemes and tactics, the less likely the potential victim has in becoming an actual victim.

Some tactical disciplines either aid or hinder successful camouflage and concealment techniques. The sensory triggers for sight and sound require proactive countermeasures to lessen the frequency of compromising your concealment.

The first thing to realize is that we are attempting to defeat an adversary (regardless of the situation) by disrupting his ability to use his senses effectively. We have five senses that the body uses to process data in the brain and as we process the information gathered through the sensory organs, we assess and determine our responses and reactions accordingly. While we have five senses, the basic elements of concealment fieldcraft are mainly trying to hinder and limit one: the sense of sight.

The sense of sight is so important to threat recognition that it sometimes causes us to focus entirely on one aspect of a threat only to miss a secondary threat or more--hence the term, *tunnel vision*, used in combat or other life-threatening situations. The sense of hearing is also used, but it only affects a few, specific stealth concepts. In the concepts using other sensory organs (i.e. the ears and nose), once the sensory organs detect something, they relinquish their power and targeting focus to the superiority of the eyes.

Human vision consists of a working combination of focal and ambient vision. Ambient vision, commonly known and referred to as peripheral vision, consists of the functions of vision associated with how objects appear in relation to their spatial orientation. The primary object detection methods are movement and contrast. Focal vision, on the other hand, is a conscious or intentional function of human eyesight, meaning it engages our brains to help identify and interpret the images transmitted from the eye. Color and shape aid our ability to rapidly interpret and discern large amounts of visual information.[1]

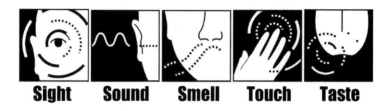

Sight   Sound   Smell   Touch   Taste

Graphic design artwork by Stephanie Hoffman. Used with permission.

To employ good stealth techniques, you must consider another's ability for keenly using their senses to detect the presence of other people. As you learn and put into practice these stealth concepts, you will have a greater understanding of how to incorporate them into your fieldcraft strategies, further enhancing your hunting or military operations. This implementation can be a formidable force multiplier when you understand the psychological effects on an adversary who cannot see or detect the force against him or the size of that force.

As humans, we have no natural colorations to employ any type of passive crypsis. Therefore, all of our crypsis methods employ active techniques, worn as articles of clothing or constructed from available materials. When we discuss detection, we are addressing the actions, behaviors, and the five senses used by individuals engaged in the detection of those using concealment techniques.

Animal vision differs from human vision in that it cannot distinguish and identify the hundreds and hundreds of color variations along the color spectrum, though birds have very keen color vision. This is not to say that animals are at some great disadvantage. Most animals have better night vision and can see some limited portions of ultraviolet light. Perhaps the easiest way to demonstrate how some animals can see ultraviolet light is with a black light.

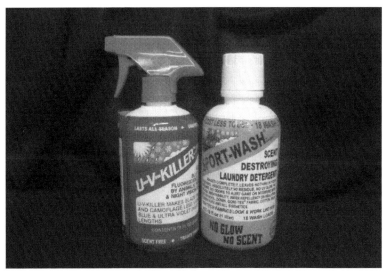

Products such as Atsko's UV Killer and Sport-Wash help reduce or eliminate the effects of ultraviolet brighteners in laundry detergents.

Most of today's laundry soaps and detergents contain ultraviolet brighteners that help keep the colors from fading. When you wash your camouflage clothing in these detergents, the same thing happens. A black light will make any color other than black appear to have a fluorescent glow. This glow is undetectable to the human eye without a black light; however, animal vision naturally detects some of the ultraviolet portion of the color spectrum. What animals lack in color vision, they more than make up for the handicap by having phenomenal senses of smell and hearing.[2] If hunting is the primary application for your camouflage and concealment endeavors, using a scent-eliminating spray or cover scent and an ultraviolet blocker will help.

When discussing the issue of scent control, it is important to have a basic understanding of the types of smells that are going to appear unnatural to the environment. Applying the S word principle, as before, here are some basic scents that most often will give your presence away to both animals and potential human adversaries:

- Soaps
- Shampoos
- Scents (colognes & perfumes)
- Spices
- Solvents (cleaners & oils)
- Sweat
- Sustenance*
- Sanitation*
- Smoke*

The last three also cross over to potential visible spoor indicators, discussed later in Chapter 8.

Game animals present another sensory challenge to deal with that greatly determines your success. In order to defeat the wariest game animals, you must defeat their sense of smell. Some predators, such as bears and wolves, can smell their prey or a carcass from more than 10 miles away in favorable weather conditions. Specialized hunting soaps and deodorants are available to help reduce human odor. Additionally, some clothing products now contain scent blocking and antimicrobial agents. Activated carbon or silver-infused clothing inhibit the various bacteria that cause body odor.

Speaking of odor, avoid foods that cause excessive gas. Beans and legumes are the most common culprits; however, individuals with lactose intolerance or other food sensitivities/allergies may have to address these considerations. If a certain food, food group, or cooking method causes your digestive tract to react contrary to good odor control, avoid it. Hunters should carefully consider the food they eat for as much as 24 hours prior to their trip into the field. If you must eat during an operation or while actively avoiding detection, choosing foods that do not require preparation (MREs) is the safest strategy against producing food odors.

Cigar and cigarette smoke can give your location away to humans up to a half-mile away with favorable weather conditions. Chronic side effects, such as coughing, will reduce your ability to remain hidden. If you are employing the use of a ghillie suit, avoid smoking due to the ghillie suit's propensity to ignite when exposed to flames and high heat sources. For this reason, most of the successful military scout sniper candidates are nonsmokers. In fact, I believe that most sniper training schools reject applications from the potential candidate pool if the applicant has a smoking habit. Despite the fact that characters portrayed by Sylvester Stallone and Arnold Schwarzenegger smoke cigars in movies, the tactical practicality of it is zero. You will become *expendable* and, most likely, *terminated* with no pithy, "I'll be back!" quote rolling off your lips.[3]

In the same manner, in cold weather, the warm air exhaled from the lungs appears as steam because of the outside air differential. This, too, can cause unwanted detection. To reduce the appearance of steam when breathing, try inhaling and exhaling through the nose only. Because the mouth is larger than the nostrils, it releases more air, faster.

Hearing is the second most important sense humans use. However, when something is unseen, sound is usually the first sense to alert us. Movement creates sound. Zero movement equals no sound. Since no movement is tactically impractical, all sound created from movement must be as quiet as possible. The more precautions taken to avoid making unnecessary or unwanted sound, the less likely your quarry will detect you. Each environment has its own unique collection of sounds, all capable of producing both challenges and advantages to the art of stealth.

A tropical rain forest may cover the sound of walking with rainfall but also increases the risk of slips and falls on wet surfaces. Forests may deflect sound vibrations by bouncing sound waves off the dense tree growth, but dried twigs and dead leaves still snap and crunch under foot. Snowy environments are even more challenging as snow and ice can cover objects that either create unwanted noises or produce a trip hazard. Ice creates all kinds of slip and fall hazards. In other environments, such as deserts or arid grasslands, you may inadvertently kick stones or rocks while walking. The lack of adequate rainfall means that visible clouds of dust may appear when walking or crawling.

The most obvious source of sound that humans have is the mouth. The mouth creates several types of sounds, but talking is the one sound that compromises people instantly. The human voice is easily identifiable to other humans, even when different languages are spoken. Animals recognize it as a sound associated with humans as well. Individuals with seasonal and outdoor allergies must also contend with the sounds produced from their bodies. Sneezing, coughing, and sniffling are sounds that uniquely identify us as human.

As a former sailor, I once had the propensity to swear frequently when tired or upset. While I might not launch into a colorful barrage of profanity, I remember to restrain my comments about biting insects or obstacles that have the tendency to snag clothing. Fieldcraft is a skill marked with patience and more patience. The practice of effective sound discipline, I believe, is essential and takes time to master. To be truly stealthy, you must be silent, with both your body and your mouth. Practicing this particular stealth concept is the only way to master it.

In addition to the sensory information used to detect others, we use a wide variety of cognitive skills. These skills involve concepts such as deduction, logic, theory, assumption, process of elimination, bias, generalization, and stereotypes, based upon the sensory information we have gathered aiding in the detection. While the scientific and philosophical explanations go far beyond my personal knowledge and expertise on the subject, it is important to know that these concepts do play a role in how we track and detect others. One of the ways I encourage people to increase their sight detection skills is by solving puzzles such as word-searches and hidden object-style games.

I have had the pleasure of speaking with renowned tactical tracking instructor, David Scott-Donelan on a handful of occasions. We both share the opinion that the greatest aid for target recognition against those using camouflage and concealment for evasion purposes is a set of binoculars. Unfortunately, in the military, this essential piece of gear is severely under issued to troops and only given to the lower officer ranks and battalion Non-Commissioned Officers (NCOs). Ideally, every soldier or Marine should be issued a compact set of binoculars. The money spent on good-quality binoculars would far benefit soldiers in combat than the cumbersome looking helmetcams.

The introduction of the helmet-cam into active combat zones may provide commanders and intelligence analysts with real-time OPINTEL, but they have done nothing to aid in the camouflaging and concealment of the devices to reduce casualties. Enemy snipers can easily range a 7 to 8 inch drop from the helmetcam to a soldier's face and adjust their aim points accordingly. Bearing that piece of information in mind, it seems that as technology improves, that the current-issue helmetcam is in dire need of a tactical upgrade as soon as it becomes available.

Spacing

Effective camouflage is void of noticeable patterns, *sections, segments, sequence,* or *symmetry*.

We are creatures of habit. We tend to perform tasks a certain way and in a certain order to increase productivity to maximize our time. We use patterns and sequences in everyday life to provide a means of order and improve productivity in certain activities. In my previous book, *Hidden Success*, I defined a pattern as an easily recognized or repeated sequence of distinguishable colors, shapes, or features. Detectable patterns in the realm of camouflage and concealment become a liability in terms of detection. Even large portions of non-patterns, such as head-to-toe matching camouflage patterns create unnatural blobs within the environment. Likewise, camouflage patterns are fashioned into uniforms. Uniform literally deconstructed into *uni-form* means one shape. When camouflage and concealment are crucial, many shapes work better than just one shape.

The purpose of eliminating patterns and sequences is to create a greater sense of randomness. This aids in blocking information receptors from gathering adequate data to identify the relative size of an object. Randomness is a difficult concept for the human mind to grasp without bias or preconceived ideas. In order to interpret large amounts of information quickly, our brains automatically set a certain amount of parameters to filter out unnecessary or irrelevant data to prevent sensory overload. This is where the concept of macro and micro patterns comes into play. Camouflage causes the human eye to have to search harder for the familiar symmetry of the human form and exposes us to more of the surrounding data in order to find objects.[1]

The octopus is the undisputed champion of adaptive, mimicry camouflage. Photo courtesy of www.pixabay.com

Most animals accomplish this through colorization, anatomy, and habitat. An example of passive crypsis is the colorations on certain species of moths or the anatomy of the stick bug. Both species have no direct control over their ability to blend into their environment. Tigers, similarly, cannot change the pattern or color of their stripes. However, when hunched down in tall grass in early dawn or dusk, they are very difficult to see. This hunting instinct is the active component, that when combined with the rising and setting sun creates the concealment, based on color and the disruptive pattern to aid in the stalking and ambush of its prey. Chameleons and anoles actively change the colorations of their skins in order to hide from predatory animals.[2]

Natural camouflage occurs in either the form of mimicry or disruption. Camouflage by means of mimicry often includes the techniques of morphology, or completely blending into the surrounding environment.[3] In all animal life, there is no greater champion in the realms of camouflage and concealment than the octopus. Octopuses have the ability to change their color, shape, and texture to morph seamlessly into their aquatic environment. At a molecular level, octopuses have chromophores, the part of a molecule that contain the pigments necessary for the octopus to change colors.[4] Not only does this make octopuses formidable predators, but also helps them avoid becoming preys themselves.

Sequence also deals with the layering of different textures or materials. For example, if you raked your fingers through the grass in your backyard, you would most likely collect the browned-out dead grass rather than uprooting the green growth. This is why I recommend individuals who utilize a ghillie suit to start with tans and browns first, then layer the green shades.

Spacing is very similar to the aspects of sequence, as it provides the breaks or repeats within the pattern. This is a concept that is easily discernible on hunting camouflage patterns. If you look at the printed pattern, you can see the spacing or the measureable, physical distance between the noticeable repeats. Most of this spacing occurs in 2 linear feet or less. For optimal effectiveness, patterns that offer spacing greater than 3 linear feet or more before the pattern repeats itself are the best. An excellent way to observe this concept is to go to a fabric store and unroll a bolt of camouflage fabric. Once rolled out, you can observe the pattern eventually repeat itself; usually within 16-24 inches, depending on the pattern.

The human body is an excellent example of relative symmetry. Because of this, we naturally look for the human outline and gravitate more to the concepts of symmetry and balance to help locate others. One thing I have learned is that pattern selection is not a fashion show. The concept of matching and coordinating is so ingrained into our thinking that we typically buy the same pattern for every article of clothing we use. This is done primarily because of the way camouflage patterns are marketed to consumers. Camouflage developers never feature another competitor's pattern alongside their own. Conducting side-by-side comparisons usually shows or exposes particular patterns' shortcomings or failure to conceal in a particular environment. Worse yet, it convinces the consumer to choose the competition's pattern, which it at odds with the whole purpose of marketing.

Mixing different patterned pants and jackets remedies this as long as the colorization blends. This aids in breaking up your profile. For example, in areas with only a light covering of snow in a wooded area, it is a common practice to wear snow cover-ups over trousers and a uniform top matching closer to the color of the trees. As one would avoid walking in an open field and would tactically move using as much natural concealment and cover as possible, this practice makes sense.

Camouflage pattern developers most likely hate this practice of non-matching camouflage, but I highly recommend it if the situation and environment allow for it. However, this tactic is not without a word of caution. This tactic only works with similar color schemes and thematic elements within the camouflage patterns. Interestingly, some elite military units allow members to wear different, non-issue camouflage on certain missions. However, as a rule, military regulations strictly prohibit this practice.

A vertical contrast within a camouflage pattern is helpful in disrupting the symmetry of the human form. This is why high-definition patterns that feature tree branches are popular. The entire purpose of introducing a tree species into a camouflage pattern is to destroy the natural appearance of human symmetry. As a result, hunters, particularly those who hunt from static positions, rely heavily on and are often successful with the infinite styles/tree species of these types of camouflage patterns. These patterns, however, lose their effectiveness when using nonstatic tactics or during nonhunting activities.

Shadow

Effective camouflage helps create shadow using the color *spectrum* and light *saturation*, while reducing the human *silhouette*.

Every object that has height and width creates shadows. The common fallacy is that shadows are black. Black, as a color, does not occur naturally in *living* plant life or vegetation. Even being overly technical and mentioning black fungi, certain types of algae or onyx, none of these examples normally create a large enough concentration to use solid color black clothing as a suitable and effective concealment consideration. The fur of black bear, black panthers, and recessive-gene timber wolves also does not provide an adequate rebuttal or defense, as the above listed animals have been hunted to the point of endangerment, with the exception of the black bear.

The existence of shadows seems to be the only defense some people have for the "black exists in nature" argument. While the majority of cast shadows can appear black, they are, in reality, darker variations of the original hues caused by the reduction of light. The object blocks the light source; thus producing shadow behind the object based upon the angle of the light source.

The unnatural shadow cast by the brims of the jungle hats. Shadow and sunlight can be very contrary to good camouflage discipline.
Photo credit: David Scott-Donelan

Black in nature exists only with the absence or reduction of light. For example, if you stand at the mouth of a cave and look in, it appears completely black. Take a flashlight and begin to walk into the cave, you see different colored rock caused by mineral deposits and erosion during cave formation. Direct sunlight will automatically expose black-colored surfaces or material. Even at night, after your eyes adjust, black can unnaturally silhouette you. If someone is looking for you with a flashlight or spotlight, blending with the natural colors of the daytime environment will work better than a SWAT uniform or ninja suit.

This does not mean that all black colorations need to be avoided, but be aware that it should be used sparingly only as a means to create the illusion of shadows and depth. I typically choose darker shades of green and brown to create the necessary shadow color tones. However, the sun will not always cooperate and will reveal shadows, despite good camouflage discipline.

One of my biggest pet peeves with some camouflage pattern developers is their insistence on developing a tactical black camouflage. The word *tactical*, when discussing black camouflage, really means "tacticool". This is because black camouflage only looks impressive and is highly visible and trackable during daylight operations. Because of this, black camouflage is far from being appropriately tactical.

This photo shows just how silhouetting black is, even when partially dressed in black. Black might work in a complete blackout, but once exposed to light, positions are compromised. Photo courtesy of www.pixabay.com

Pattern developers who have established themselves in the tactical LEO markets have me shaking a clench-fisted hand in the air and scratching my head with the other in what appears to be an effort to sell more products. This is not the case with some pattern developers, but my greatest concern regarding this subject is police and SWAT officer safety.

I have talked with some of these camouflage developers regarding their respective black camouflage patterns. Oftentimes, the main issue comes down to supplying metropolitan police departments with uniforms and gear that does not require departments to replace tactical equipment, load-bearing equipment, plate carriers, and pouches that still are in good operating condition. Most metropolitan police departments and municipalities issue black or blue colored uniforms. Those who hold the department's financial purse strings often validate the issuance of solid black tactical gear is because of its lower price and its ability to color coordinate with a wider variety of uniform colors. While I do not agree with the choice, I empathize with the budget constraints. From my observations, sheriff departments seem to have greater latitude with camouflage choices, most likely because they are more likely to find themselves in rural environments.

The shadow and silhouette cast by the human body is amplified and much more detectable when wearing solid black or black dominant camouflage. Even with an implied nocturnal operational component, obtaining greater concealment is possible with a camouflage pattern suited and matched to the daytime operational environment. Our own military already know the drawbacks of black in camouflage patterns. All of our military branches have moved away from the once popular M85 Woodland Camouflage pattern with its large black patches incorporated throughout the pattern. Even the miniscule amounts of black in the desert camouflage (dubbed the "chocolate chip" pattern) used during the first Gulf War and the Liberation of Kuwait, were enough to convince top brass to move to patterns that removed all of the black colorations from present and future camouflage patterns.

When you throw in the infrared (IR) component and thermal detection technology of the modern military and police agencies, black camouflage potentially becomes a major liability to mission success. Black uniforms, absorb light waves and heat and then trap that absorbed heat onto the wearer's body. The body's emissivity then reflects that heat back to the optical eyes of today's thermal detection devices.

There are two spectrums affecting the human senses, the color spectrum affecting the sense of sight and the sound spectrum affecting our hearing. Because we use our sense of sight primarily for detection, identification, and classification, I will address the color spectrum first. Sound will be addressed later, as it relates to and affects the concept of shifting and movement.

The human eye can detect and differentiate hundreds and hundreds of color variations. The variations are almost innumerable, and they quickly change based upon weather conditions, time of day, and season. Take a notepad and a pencil/pen and write down the different things you see in your environment. Describe it by color, height, width, shape, and anything that will help you accurately reproduce the colorations. A color wheel or an offset printer's color guide will help give you an idea of the varying shades and different colors to use on your ghillie suit. Compare your notes with color swatches from your local paint or home improvement store and then match those colors to those in a selected camouflage pattern. The better you can identify specific colors in your operating environment, the more effective your camouflage choice.

Colors used to create camouflage should not be limited to the conventional brown and green tones. Do not forget that variations of yellows, reds, and even blues, along with differing shades of grey add to the overall effectiveness of camouflage.

Here is something to consider about camouflage pattern choice. Any pattern that has more browns than any other color works the best. With the four seasons in consideration, brown colors blend in a majority of the time. When choosing a camouflage pattern, it is best to shop where you can see the pattern and color in person. It doesn't mean you should buy it where you look at it, but at least allow yourself to view the pattern with your eye in natural light to avoid being persuaded by marketing photos in catalogs and on online sites. Photographers use every enhancement at their disposal to make the patterns appear to melt into the landscape, creating an illusion of invisibility to sell the product. What they cannot manipulate through natural techniques, they manipulate with photo editing software like Adobe Photoshop and other similar programs.

Just as color spectrum is important, the texture of certain materials used for camouflage and concealment also affects the color. My high school art teacher often reminded her students to experiment with textures to achieve different color variations.

Thi s photo depicts how egregious the effects of sky-lining against a lit background or horizon can be, even when wearing a ghillie suit. Photo credit: Tech Sgt. Efren Lopez, USAF. The appearance of U.S. Department of Defense (DoD) visual information does not imply or constitute DoD endorsement.

A silhouette is the result of an object being backlit by a light source or the object obscuring a portion of a light source. Major John Plaster (USAR ret.) and other snipercraft instructors refer to this as skylining.[1] Silhouette refers to the outline or profile of an object. This concept closely relates to shape in the sense that the silhouette of a person defines the shape of that person. The silhouette and outline of the body is the single greatest identifier of the human form, as shown in the previous photo. Anything that breaks up the fluid lines of the human silhouette often provides better concealment and reduces detection. The ghillie suit specifically addresses the task of obscuring the human silhouette.

Another aspect of skylining comes into play, especially in surveillance scenarios. When an object impedes observation, it is best to look around the object instead of over it. The head and shoulders are the most noticeable feature that humans look for when actively searching for others.[2]

Shine

Effective camouflage reduces or eliminates *skin* reflections, *sheen*, and *shimmer*, while disrupting, dispersing, or dissipating IR, thermal *sensors*, and *signatures*.

Shine refers to an object's ability or inability to reflect or refract light off itself. Shine is highly dependent upon the angle of the sun and requires careful monitoring, especially in static positions or hides. At one point of the day, it could be overcast and then clear and sunny the next. While the sun's angle will produce shadows from one direction, it will create glares on another. Any number of manmade objects can produce shine and reflections, most often items that are flat and metal are the culprits of unwanted shine. Therefore, it is critical to reduce unwanted shine from your person and your gear. The most common shine culprits are metal, glass, and plastics. Objects that collect moisture, or produce moisture such as human skin, also tend to reflect sunlight.

Most shine issues on your person stem from liquid on the skin or your skin tone does not blend into the environment. Perspiration and the body's natural oils produce a reflective sheen. Even among Middle Eastern ethnicities and those with African heritage, there is a need to be aware of the effects of shine. Using military or civilian face paint helps reduce shine from exposed skin areas. One of the products I highly recommend is Carbomask, a hypoallergenic cream that utilizes the scent blocking properties of activated carbon. Unlike other face paints, Carbomask comes in a wide variety of different shades and washes off with just water. Carbomask does not feel as heavy or noticeable on your face compared to other camouflage face paints and is my go-to choice and recommendation for camouflaging facial features.

Carbomask face paint colors, from left to right, Shadow Black, Hunter Green, Earth Brown, Wolf Gray, Sagebrush Green, and Desert Tan.
Photo credit: BAHSpence/www.carbomask.com

The common school of thought regarding camouflage face paint application is that the protruding areas of the face should be darker and the recessed areas lighter in color. This helps produce a reversal in the contrast polarity of the face. The protruding areas of the face are the nose, forehead, chin, and cheekbones. The recessed areas are the eye sockets, inner ears, neck, and lower jawbone. One thing to remember, avoid making a symmetrical pattern where both sides of the face have a similar appearance. Applying diagonal lines eliminates facial symmetry and is a blending compromise between having a more noticeable vertical or horizontal design on the face.

Improvised kill-flashes make with coffee straws and duct tape. This technique works in effectively reducing glints and reflections off the optic lenses of binoculars and telescopic sights.

All of the gear and supplies most people take out with them into the field are manmade goods. These goods, made in factories from processed materials, have no occurrence in or link to nature other than the natural resources used to make those products. It is imperative to conceal the manmade appearance. To combat the negative aspects of shine on gear, spray paint is often used. The luster or finish of the paint is important aspect, just as much as the color. The best finishes are flat, ultra-flat or matte finishes. Avoid semi-gloss and gloss finishes because they have a greater tendency to reflect light.

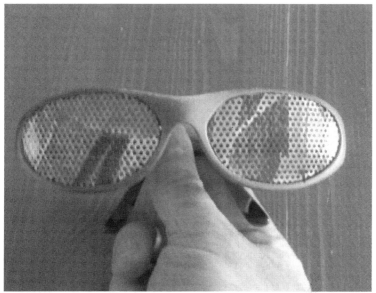

Eyeglasses and sunglasses can produce glares and reflections counter to good concealment discipline. I modified an old pair of prescription sunglasses by spray painting the frames with rubberized spray paint and sticking perforated window film with a camo print pattern on the lenses to reduce some of the unwanted reflection. Vision is slightly reduced, but the symmetry of the lenses is broken up.

If your budget allows for it, there are specialized spray paints that block UV light and dampen the effects of RADAR. There are also ceramic-based paints that claim to have thermal reduction qualities, as well.

While this photo shows the proper reduction of shine from the skin, the improperly camouflaged weapons can compromise one's position. Why does the government continue to request black colored weapons when protective coatings like Cerakote and hydrographic dipping are available? Photo credit: David Scott-Donelan

The stealth concept of signature refers to the heat signature produced by the human body. The heat your body gives off is detectable through infrared (IR) and thermal imaging technology. To be clear, it is necessary to understand that a thermal barrier is *not* a thermal absorbent. While there are signature reduction technologies available to the military, there are very few effective, unclassified countermeasures currently available to civilians to defeat these technologies. However, certain types of concealment deflect, reflect, or absorb heat emissions from the body.

To avoid any confusion as to how we visually or mechanically/electronically detect electromagnetic waves, we must understand where the infrared, visible light and ultraviolet spectrums are in relation to each other in the overall electromagnetic spectrum.

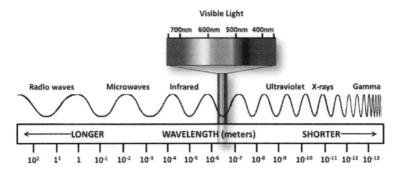

A basic representation of the electromagnetic spectrum.[1]

Another form of imaging developed after World War II is CIR (color infrared) photography. This produces a false color photograph (digital or celluloid film) where the object's true or natural colors are rendered into the RGB (red, green, blue) spectrum for analysis. This was developed primarily to detect camouflage netting used by enemy forces to camouflage equipment. Living plants give of a noticeable differential of infrared waves compared to diseased, dying, or dead vegetation. Based upon the vegetation's NIR (near infrared) reflectance, Living vegetation appears as bright red, stressed vegetation (from drought or disease shows up in a darker red and all other terrain or objects in the photograph would have colorations based upon its organic composition.[2]

While the use of CIR is normally for agricultural and land management purposes, most commonly in the form of aerial photography, the method is applicable and effective at any camera angle. With it is conceivable that this technology could be used to detect individuals attempting

45

to conceal themselves. The development of certain fabric and paint additives used on current military-style netting allow the effectiveness of this technology to be somewhat diminished.

Prototype model of an IR/thermal reduction ghillie cloak. Photo credit: www.snakebitetactical.com

Some methods of thermal and infrared reduction are cumbersome, bulky, and very hot. These methods often require practitioners to wrap themselves in insulation or some other kind of radiant barrier material. Despite the bulkiness and heat, these types of IR and thermal signature reduction tactics do work, as proven by a YouTube video entitled, *Defeating Drones: How to Build a Thermal Evasion Suit*, presented by Oath Keepers.[3] The same video is featured on the Snakebite Tactical website as well.

I contacted Brandon Smith of Snakebite Tactical and asked him a couple of questions about his IR/thermal reduction design. He did state that the suit generates no more heat than that of a standard ghillie suit, so indeed, the suits are inherently warm. While there is a required construction method that must be adhered to, the video proof provided on the Snakebite Tactical website is undeniable.

Even on the most sensitive thermal setting on the FLIR (forward-looking infrared) device, there was, as promised, at least a 90% reduction in heat emission from the wearer. However, despite the effectiveness of IR and thermal reduction suits, governments and military forces will continue to develop technologies for both defeating and detecting individual thermal reduction/elimination tactics, both on the battlefield and for homeland security.

Until the first quarter of 2016, there was an Austrian company manufacturing VIS/NIR garlands that successfully defeated infrared detection. The company was called Organic Look, but at the time of this printing, it appears that they are no longer in operation. I hope that the technology becomes available through another channel. There are only a handful of pictures of the product left on the internet and featured in a few YouTube videos.

In terms of natural camouflage, organic materials-- such as clay, dry soil, powdered charcoal, and wood ash-- can dull down some of the UV brighteners in clothing, and also reduce shine and skin reflections. The fresher the wood ash the better, as wood ash with long exposure to water can cause the ash to become caustic and cause chemical burns.[4]

One of the more bizarre ways I have discovered to reduce reflectance in the NIR spectrum is spraying down your uniform with Aqua Net hair spray. This has shown to be effective in closely matching background reflectance levels. There is also a NIR absorbing dye available from Fabric Holding, Inc., but it does noticeably change the color of the camouflage pattern/uniform in the visual spectrum.[5]

Shifting

Effective camouflage aids in the execution of *stealth* movement, including the elements of *stalking*, *speed*, *stillness*, and *stride*.

Movement always triggers a response that is impossible to eliminate. Without movement, it is difficult to engage most targets. The need for mobility requires careful, thought-out planning. Many times, the luxury of slowly meandering at a casual pace is not offered to us by operational mandates and protocols. We are often on strict time lines to reach objectives and checkpoints, requiring us to move at a pace that can create more opportunities to make unwanted sounds. The need to travel under the cover of darkness exponentially creates more opportunities for potential detection.

Movement results in detection when the concepts of speed and stillness are not applied properly to the terrain. Take advantage of both cover and concealment to make large body motions or traversing large expanses of land. Of all the concepts, stealth or movement is the concept that often reveals and compromises any concealment endeavor.

Speed, in the realms of a concept of camouflage, is an oxymoron. Nothing regarding stealth movement is done in excess, fast, or without some premeditation. The key is keeping any movement minimal, planned, and slow. Rapid movement is much easier to notice, even peripherally. Excess movement creates noise and lengthens the time your motions are vulnerable to detection. Movement should also be fluidly swift, not choppy. Too many starts and stops in your movement create more opportunity for visual detection. Planning your movements and your routes prevent or lessen the likelihood of finding yourself with little or no cover.

One of the simplest ways to practice stealth movement is by learning how to "fox walk". Renowned primitive survivalist and tracker, Tom Brown III, describes the basics of the fox walk in a video post on YouTube.[1] First, the knees are bent slightly to lower the center of gravity. Second, your stride must be reduced from your standard gait in order to maintain balance and to allow your feet to "feel" the ground and any objects or obstacles underfoot. Third, your footfall starts with the outer ball of your foot contacting the ground first, and then rolling inward until your entire body weight is supported. Finally, the opposite foot applies the same technique, and so on and so on.

Another concept of speed that warrants some attention is wind speed. When it comes to stealth and concealment, wind speed provides some distinct advantages. First, rustling leaves and grasses can disguise some of the noise generated by your movements. About the only time wind speed is not an advantage, is when snipers are trying to take critical shots, as the whole gamut from gentle breezes to gusty winds affect bullet trajectory and point of impact.

Just as movement causes detection, the lack of movement also draws an adversary's attention to a static object within an otherwise dynamic environment. While blowing wind is often not considered a dynamic variable unless employed as a sniper, it can play a crucial role in concealment. Wind speed has also been the downfall of individuals who solely rely on two-dimensional, high-definition camouflage patterns. The patterns have great representations of various tree species with all the right colorations on the leaves, but the printed leaves fail to react appropriately to the promptings of the wind.

This becomes a good focal point for locating others when there is adequate wind to generate leaf movement. It is possible for some leaves to be protected from wind by natural obstacles or other branches of the tree canopy, reducing their movement. However, motionless leaves are an indicator of two-dimensional camouflage clothing.

Stillness within your environment is heavily dependent upon your body positioning and how comfortable you are in that position. Comfort, however, is not always a luxury one can afford, especially if the given comfort compromises your position. Most often, the prone position reduces the profile more effectively than standing or crouching. An important thing to remember is you must retain the ability to see from your concealed position.

Footprints offer a vast amount of information about a pursuant. While confusing or throwing off an expert tracker is difficult to do, you can slow them down and provide less information they can use while tracking you over long distances. The easiest way to do this is by varying your stride. Concentrating on how your foot falls while walking allows you to adjust how the impressions are left in the soil. However, this tactic is often more mentally taxing and is maintainable only for short distances before lapsing back into your regular stride. It is impossible to eliminate footprints.

Certain weather conditions hold distinct advantages, as well as disadvantages for most trackers. Dry conditions allow most tracks in loose soil and sand to remain visible and relatively detailed. Strong rainstorms can erase some major features from footprints, but maintain the overall size of the foot.

One of the most notable and notorious tactics used by illegal immigrants attempting to cross the border into the United States is "carpet shoes". Several of my tracking associates report that many individuals strap irregularly shaped pieces of carpet to the bottom of their shoes to disguise their footprints. It is not exclusive to illegal immigrants, but drug cartels and the "mules" they employ or force to transport illegal drugs and other contraband across unsecured portions of the border use this tactic, as well. In an OSI camouflage and concealment video from the 1990s featuring renowned tracker, David Scott-Donelan, he referred to these booties as Stock-Mocs. I've tried to look for them online to see if they are still available commercially, but have had little success. Any technique used to disguise or eliminate footprints will also play an important role in regards to sign and spoor. This will be explained further in Chapter 8 when discussing surroundings.

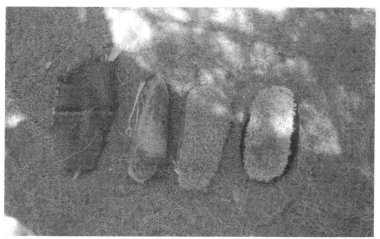

Samples of carpet shoes used by illegal aliens and drug mules to thwart tracking efforts on the Arizona-Mexico border. Photo credit: www.azborderdefenders.org

Oftentimes, your stride is less about the physical act of walking and more about how noticeable of a trail you create as you move. This may be walking or crawling, depending on the terrain and the other stealth tactics you employ. When utilizing group movements, it is essential to add synchronization to your movement strategies.

Moving while trying to maintain concealment is a skill that requires practice before any manifestation of expertise or perfection exists. The terrain and weather conditions often dictate how fast or how slow one travels. Large, open terrain takes longer to cross when attempting to maintain concealment. Under normal circumstances, quite the opposite is true. Rocky terrain, while more treacherous, provides more concealment opportunities. However, being stuck at a particular point exposes you to detection.

Surface

Effective camouflage disrupts or interferes with an adversary's ability to judge *size*, *shape*, and *structures*.

Nothing in nature is truly flat or straight. Therefore, minimizing surface areas that attract attention is a necessity. Surface is a concealment concern inter-related to shine, shape, and size. While both flat and rounded objects can produce reflections, another point of concern is an object's ability to radiate heat off its surface. This is where detection technologies--such as radar, thermal imaging, and infrared--become a major game-changer. The larger and flatter an object is, the more heat it generates on its surface area. Therefore, manmade angles and shapes need something to break up their appearance and dissipate absorbed heat. Hot surfaces generate heat waves detectable to the human eye. With the added technology of thermal emission detection, detection is almost inevitable unless using countermeasures to reduce the surface area and details of certain structures and essential gear.

Humans have a distinct size and proportion. This concept is important to address because of our mobility. Because movement attracts attention, altering or concealing our size, can cause adversaries to overlook certain movement, landscape features and natural cover, only if we make our size appear too small to disguise the human form.

For example, a large boulder measuring over three square feet easily covers and conceals someone hiding behind it. However, a one square foot fieldstone often does not adequately conceal someone behind it. Larger objects within the landscape draw our attention simply because they are much easier to see. Smaller objects are much more difficult to observe. When you add the factor of distance to an object, it becomes more apparent that the larger the object, the easier it is to see.

A training exercise on the southern border of Arizona and Mexico utilizing a ghillie blanket with artificial rocks. It blends seamlessly within the rocky terrain. Photo credit: Shawn Swanson

Therefore, you will want to make yourself smaller by incorporating tactics that appear to obscure your human size. These include tactics of adding material or using a ghillie suit that can deceive someone based upon the relative size of other objects around you. In rocky terrain, I like to use fake rocks and stones. A simple fake stone made from a brown paper bag, masking tape, and some artistic application of textured spray paint with an approximate diameter of 8 - 10 inches weighs less than 3 ounces. However, a real stone of that size might weigh 20 pounds or more. Another method uses shaped, high-density foam coated with lightweight Hydrocal plaster and then painted to match the appropriate rock formations. It is a time-consuming technique and requires regular upkeep, but it can really pay off it terms of personal camouflage.

There are certain shapes that reveal whether or not is something manmade or occurring in nature. Perfect circles and straight lines are dead giveaways to the presence of something man-made. For example, outfitting yourself in a complete ghillie suit, with a weapon system painted in subdued colors is a great start. However, if you fail to break up the outline of the perfectly round objective bell of a riflescope, the protective flip cover, or the barrel, you could easily compromise your position. Here are the three key S words concerning shape:

- Straight lines
- Squares
- Sphericals

Abstract patterns in camouflage create visual disruptions for the observer. However, the abstract shapes within the pattern should not contain large or unnatural shapes. Objects with or portions of straight lines, right angles, perfect circles, eclipses or other geometric shapes not occurring naturally within a particular environment are detection flags that will compromise your position.

Despite having an A-TACS hydrographic coating, this objective lens cap still retains its familiar spherical/circular shape and is one of the things to look for when counter-sniping. When the cap is open, now there are two perfectly round objects stacked next to each other. The second photo shows a small rare earth magnet epoxied to the interior of the cap.

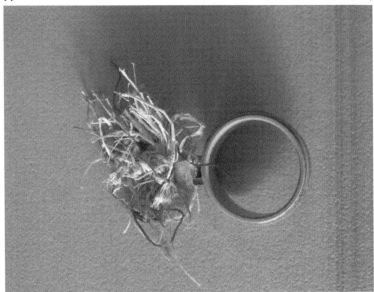

A piece of Cordura scrap with a second rare earth magnet sewn into a miniature pocket and then adorned with raffia grass and other ghillie material to conceal half of the open lens cap. Using a rubber band around the other portion allows the user to insert grasses to break up the outline a little more. Rotating the cap to the five or seven o'clock position helps as well.

The shape and symmetry of the human head is probably the most detectable feature of the body. Since humans are bipeds, walking erect in the full height of our stature most of the time, this is a key detection feature. There are three ways we typically try to disrupt the outline of our head. First, we wear a hat of some sort. While many different hat styles come in a wide variety of camouflage patterns, some hats work better than others for concealment purposes. The best overall hat for camouflage and concealment is the jungle hat, commonly referred to as a boonie hat. Adorning the vegetation loops of a boonie hat with natural foliage or ghillie material and allowing that material to drape over the brim effectively disrupts some of the shape and symmetry of the head.

This photo of the author, shown with his head exposed (top) and then covered with a ghillie headnet (bottom), demonstrates the necessity to conceal not only shine, but shape as well. With the head exposed, one can discern most of his body proportions.

The second method of head shape and symmetry reduction is the use of the previously mentioned face paints. There are those, who chose to use a Spandex headnet marketed as Spando-flage to conceal their face. In reality, this product only helps reduce the shine from the wearer's skin. The material's characteristic ability to conform to the wearer's shape actually makes the head shape, symmetry, and spherical appearance much more pronounced. While it may be faster to don, there are better choices, in my opinion.

The third head concealment method is a loose-fitting, mesh headnet or bag. The head and neck are covered effectively, while vision is only partially reduced. This method is also helpful to those who wear corrective eyeglasses. The fabric folds of the mesh break up the head shape and users have the added benefit of keeping biting insects away. Swatting at annoying insects is a very noticeable movement to detect, especially as patience is a key factor. Not everyone is a SEAL, Force Recon, or Green Beret who can sit still for twelve hours while mosquitoes dine at will and eventually die of gluttony or sheer exhaustion from trying to annoy a victim who is unwilling to give any response.

My best advice is to incorporate all three methods to break up head shape and symmetry, or at the very least, two. Using only one method is not nearly as effective as two or three.

One of my favorite things to observe are beginners, especially in airsoft and paintball games, attempting to employ the sole use of a ghillie suit. They typically use a store-bought, cheap Chinese garment of limited/poor coloration with no additional local foliage to aid its effectiveness. Secondly, these young people will come out to the field with a brand-spanking-new airsoft rifle with a pristine black satin finish. I may have a harder time detecting the individual in a ghillie suit, but because of my knowledge of basic weapon shapes and styles, my attention for detecting the individual now focuses on the concepts I can detect: the shape of his weapon and his protective gear.

This airsoft protective mask has a camo-printed perforated window film adhered to the lens and ghillie material attached via netting to break up the shape and surface of the mask.

This goes even further by recognizing the shapes of other essential field gear like packs, and helmets. Modular Lightweight Load-bearing Equipment (MOLLE, pronounced Molly) is great for modular-based equipment carriers. However, the mounting straps on tactical vests and plate carriers run in perfect parallel. This goes back to straight lines and squares mentioned earlier in the chapter. To reduce the straight lines and squares, weave some vegetation or ghillie material through any unused straps to break up the outline of any gear. This does create some functional limitations, and hinders pouch access to a certain degree, so try finding a workable compromise between concealment and gear access.

One surface that I particularly have to pay attention to in my camouflage and concealment tactics are my eyeglasses. Eyeglasses are notorious for their reflective surfaces and their smooth, manmade lines and symmetry. While the best option is not to wear eyeglasses and opt for contact lenses, I use perforated window film to reduce glare on an old pair of prescription sunglasses (seen on page 43). It does not eliminate all surface glares, but it does reduce a reasonable amount and also reduces the brightness of the sun. This application is also suitable for paintball and airsoft protective masks.

Surroundings

Effective camouflage will blend in with the *seasons*, *scenery*, and environment, while the wearer proactively eliminates detectable *sign* and *spoor*.

As humans, we must use active camouflaging techniques, deliberately taking steps to conceal our location and ourselves. Knowing how to hide and where to hide is a lot like real estate. Everything is about location, location, location! Depending on the particular application, especially those in military and law enforcement roles, one must also plan for an escape contingency. The best hide location is of little value if easily discovered or advanced on by hostile forces. Hiding requires thoughtful discretion, avoiding lone landmarks or landscape features that draw the attention of an observer, sentry, or patrol. This is usually the downfall of inexperienced or untrained practitioners of fieldcraft.

Blending in is about matching textures, shapes, and even smells--not just colors. The dichotomy of camouflage is that we must use tangible objects and materials to create the illusion of intangibility. We use fabrics and natural vegetation, not to look like *those* materials, but to look like the surroundings. The ultimate goal is to look like nothing at all, because it is possible to blend into the surroundings with the right colors and vegetation, yet detectable because we appear as a large unnatural clump of something that sticks out amongst the natural terrain.

In order to be 100% effective, any camouflage and concealment effort must blend into the surroundings. Photo credit: Shawn Swanson.

Among the more interesting camouflage developments I have found is Cabela's Zonz Warm and Cold Phase camouflage patterns. While it is only offered in the pattern's Woodland and Western configurations, it truly is an innovative concept. The brown and green portions of the camouflage pattern actually change color based on the temperature. Color transition occurs at approximately 65°F (18°C). I didn't believe it myself, until I watched a product review. While it would not work in every environment, the concept is great for those who only want to buy one set of camouflage hunting clothing. This is a product, if properly conceived and executed, could have some major implications in both the military and civilian camouflage markets in the future.[1]

Another way your camouflage subject matter compromises itself within an environment is by polarization. Polarization is a term I use to describe occurrences where something within a camouflage pattern creates an unnatural focal point. There are four ways that camouflage patterns become polarized are by color, orientation, object, or behavioral.[2]

In my previous book, *Hidden Success*, I made a brief mention of the principle of behavioral orientation, but did not define as such at the time. As I mentioned earlier in the introduction, I am always learning new things and try to pass them on to other camouflage enthusiasts and practitioners. Sharing knowledge is always my go-to policy, unless there are established protocols in place dealing with national security, operational security (OPSEC), or the good, old-fashioned element of "need-to-know".

Color Polarization

Color polarization is similar to the appearance of a negative exposure photograph. Portions that should appear dark appear light and vice versa. This is the downfall of almost all snow or winter camouflage patterns. Traditional urban camouflage originally marketed as SnowFlage, suffers from the overuse of black and grey in its color scheme making the pattern ineffective in winter environments.[3] Later versions replaced the grey color with a brown, but still failed because the black and brown portions were still too large. Other civilian snow patterns fail to solve the problem as well. Most have white backgrounds with layered tree limbs and leaves. Designers fail to take into account that snow covers or clings to stationary objects. Color polarization also occurs when using a green dominant camouflage in a desert environment and vice versa.[4]

Orientation Polarization

This refers to the implied position or direction that the pattern runs through the garment, commonly referred to as horizontal, vertical or diagonal. Trees, grasses, and bushes all grow vertically and the shadows they cast often run the same way or at varying angles.

The very natural, organic vertical orientation is the most common in most environments. The horizontal orientation of some camouflage patterns would stand out, increasing the possibility of detection. Photo courtesy of www.pixabay.com

Therefore, patterns like the Vietnam-era Tiger-Stripe camouflage polarize themselves with a horizontal orientation that contradicts the dominant vertical orientation of most shadows and vegetation growth. Despite its marginal effectiveness, most tiger-stripe patterns are still popular. Tiger-stripe camouflage would be more effective if it offered both vertical and horizontal orientations throughout the pattern.[5]

Object Polarization

Object polarization refers to anything within the camouflage pattern that appears unnatural or out of place. Many people have thought they had blended perfectly into their surroundings, but were then caught by the game warden because their camouflage clothing had leaves that did not move in the wind or had pinecones on oak trees. Game wardens, law enforcement personnel, and counter-snipers are highly trained to detect people hunters and poachers with these types of detection flags.[2]

Behavioral Polarization

Stationary objects (e.g., tree limbs, rocks, stones, boulders) are for static locations and sniper hides. The larger the objects you use for your hide or ghillie suit, the more stationary your suit and/or your position becomes. This is where the static/dynamic elements of active camouflage come into play. These static/dynamic elements create behavioral polarization. Simply put, objects should or should not behave, respond or react in ways that are contrary to their natural design and intrinsic properties and characteristics. For example, on a windy day, you should expect to see leaves and branches naturally responding to the blow of the breeze. Likewise, you should not expect to see a rock or log moving unaided, as this violates the natural laws of gravity, motion, and force.

Some popular camouflage patterns unfortunately polarize themselves against the environment. Camouflage patterns, especially newer, high-definition patterns are the primary focus of the Subject concept, especially when discussing the topic of polarization. Take care when purchasing a camouflage pattern from commercial brands (such as Mossy Oak and Realtree) for use on a ghillie suit. Many of these common hunting camouflage patterns work well. This is not necessarily the result of well-conceived patterns, but rather the wearer's ability to learn and implement good field tactics, remaining motionless and quiet. These patterns work very well for hunters as they blend in well in environments that have only a few dominant types of vegetation and are static or non-moving in design. However, it is a good thing that animals cannot read. Most of these patterns have their brand name printed all over the garment. If you are hiding from humans, someone with a spotting scope might be able to read these off your clothes. If you choose to wear such patterns, there are ways to solve this problem.[7]

High-definition camouflage is created with a blurred or solid color background with obscured objects in the mid-ground and highly detailed, photo-quality images of leaves, branches, and tree bark in the foreground. Most of these high-definition patterns are for use in static positions like tree stands or fallen timber. Sniper crawling in one of these patterns would look like a migrating pile of logs and leaves. Some of these patterns may work great for your particular hunting environment. However, if you are involved in paintball or airsoft games and the game field has a variety of different vegetation, I would avoid these patterns. The problem is apparent when trying to adapt single-environment patterns to multi-environment playing fields; the pattern will fail you--miserably.[8]

Another aspect of high-definition camouflage is the blatant dichotomy of purpose. High-definition, by its inherent design, provides a crisp, clear, *defining* representation of the intended surroundings. Therefore, it is not trying to confuse the eye with out-of-focus or abstract objects, but rather mimic the surrounding foliage. These artistic details, reduce the need for our eyes to try to decipher what we are looking at and turn our focus to how it supposed to react and respond within the environment. While the camouflage patterns will certainly mimic the appearance of the foliage, the pattern cannot mimic its behavior.

The biggest problem I have found with these patterns is that they contain leaves. The artwork is great, amazingly realistic in color, scale, and detail. The key element the designers cannot reproduce is the fact that leaves move in the breeze, a prime example of behavioral polarization. Another design flaw that hinders the effectiveness of high-definition camouflage patterns for anti-personnel camouflage are the close proximity of varying tree species within a space where the differing species would not or could not occupy in a natural setting. You can refer back to the photo in Chapter 1 to refresh your memory on the disadvantages of high-definition camouflage patterns.

Another thing often overlooked is the content of ghillie suits. While many ghillie suits do an excellent job matching colors and varying textures to match the environment, a significant number look like huge clumps of string and thread. Another fellow ghillie suit and concealment aficionado, Nate Turner, put it this way. "Ghillie suits, especially the store-bought ones from China, end up looking like 'spaghillie', a spaghetti-inspired, tangled mess".

Spoor is a word we do not commonly use in America, but the average hunter knows it by definition. Spoor is anything an animal leaves behind as evidence that it, at one time, occupied that particular place. Americans, typically refer to spoor as "sign" of a quarry's presence at a particular location. This evidence typically includes tracks, fur, or droppings (scat).

As humans, we leave behind a large amount of physical evidence regarding spoor. Fortunately, the strict adherence to the practice of "good housekeeping" disciplines eliminates a good majority of these clues. I will use the term *trash* and break the general term down to the three basic trash/spoor types: food, human waste, and fire. Here again, using S words, we can identify and categorize three spoor/sign types:

- Sustenance
- Sanitation
- Smoke

If you remember, these three identifiers have implications relating to the sense of smell, discussed in Chapter 2.

People, especially Americans, throw away copious amounts of trash. Finding trash littered upon trails, along roads and highways or anywhere else where there is relative seclusion or the lack of a trash receptacle is a key indicator of human presence. Not only is it unsightly, it also gives the opposition physical clues similar to jigsaw puzzle pieces that allow a pursuer to detect or discover your location. It is like leaving a trail of breadcrumbs right to your hide location or favorite hunting spot.

Food waste is the most common, simply because of its prevalence and ease of discovery. The bright colors of candy bar wrappers, soup cans and even the subdued colors of a meal, ready-to-eat (MRE) bag can catch the eye of anyone determined to find you. The smells of food waste attract insects and animals, which in most cases, are unwanted. This becomes increasingly important in areas with large predators and scavengers.

When discussing human waste, sealing bodily evacuations in plastic bags or bottles and taking them with you for disposal at an appropriate facility is the preferred method. There are times when such action is neither practical nor tactical; therefore, burial is the best field expedient disposal method. It reduces detection by canine units when buried deep enough (12-16 inches minimum) and leaves nothing for trackers or pursuers to analyze. As objectionable as it might sound, several factors regarding current diet and intestinal health can be ascertained by careful examination of discovered bowel movement evidence.

Fire spoor is simply evidence or remnants of a warming fire, cooking fire, or both. Improvised fire pits, ash piles, charred wood, charcoal, and browned out areas from intense heat are all dead giveaways to a recent fire.

The other major signs both animals and humans leave behind are footprints. An experienced tracker can determine with a reasonable amount of accuracy, the height, weight, and stride of the pursuant. Injuries affecting a person's gait are also identifiable by a good tracker. Stealth movement, including the topic of concealing tracks and footprints are explained back in Chapter 6 on Shifting.

Status Quo

Effective urban camouflage morphs into the accepted apparel choices of *society*, ensuring that clothing maintains anonymity, *secrecy*, and *security* in urban *scenarios*.

Society, in general, thrives on status quo, conformity, and order. At least, that is the desired intention. More and more each day, we see the result of both the overt and covert attempts of societal norms and the powers that perpetrate them to persuade us to comply and conform. Unfortunately, our world is becoming increasingly more dangerous and our rights to defend ourselves and maintain a comfortable level of privacy are eroding at an alarming rate.

Despite this, society attempts to maintain a semblance of civility and the illusion that nothing has changed. In nature, change occurs slowly, so it appears to be unchanging. That is the goal endeavored by individuals yearning to disappear. Everything done must appear to have been undisturbed, unchanged, and unaffected by your presence. In an urban setting, everything becomes a dynamic, sometimes chaotic, ever-changing environment.

73

No book on the subject of camouflage and concealment would be complete without addressing the need to blend into urban settings. This means that traditional camouflage patterned apparel featuring strict vegetative and earth colors is no longer appropriate and actually draws attention in the urban environment. While we attempt to keep a vigilant eye out for things out of the ordinary, we must keep from drawing undue or extra attention to ourselves.

This chapter may not seem as important compared to the other chapters, but the reason for its inclusion is paramount for those who may find themselves in a situation of trying to navigate through and/or escape from an area of civil unrest or curfew enforcements due to a declaration of martial law. This is not a guide or an avocation for illegal activity or civil disobedience. In these types of situations, many people attempt to practice what is commonly referred to as the "gray man" concept.

The intention behind the "gray man" is to disappear within a crowd. The practitioner dons clothing, mannerisms, and a demeanor that does not draw attention to him or herself. He or she does not want to be recognizable, identifiable, or memorable. Therefore, the camouflage paradigm must transition from the realms of rural remoteness to the populated urban environment.

When crossing over from a more rural/woodland setting to an urban environment, you need a camouflage pattern that transitions effectively into the new surroundings. While there have been urban camouflage patterns developed, the colorations have been the only noticeable change. In cities and towns, solid colors blend into more areas, without compromising or limiting oneself to a particular area of an urban environment.

It is also important to remember that buildings and structures within any given city are all manmade with hard, geometrically precise, straight lines and angles. Nothing from an architectural standpoint is random or natural. Everything manmade is designed, detailed, and meticulously thought out to a certain degree of functionality. In the urban environment, straight lines are natural, welcomed, and expected. Your clothing choices should try to accommodate this mantra.

The first key to blending into an urban setting is clothing. Brightly colored clothing (or nakedness, for that matter) is highly detectable and allows pursuers to key in on you and your movements. Depending on the situation, when your apparel displays team logos, trademarks, and other notable features, your ability to disappear into a crowd considerably decreases. One of the few places where this is not an issue would be at a sporting event.

These are not new techniques or concepts, as the Central Intelligence Agency (CIA), Drug Enforcement Agency (DEA), Bureau of Alcohol, Tobacco, & Firearms (ATF), and the Federal Bureau of Investigations (FBI) all teach this form of clandestine fieldcraft to their agents. Whether the agent's job is to follow a foreign agent, masquerade as a client of illegal contraband, or to run surveillance on suspects, they all must blend in, in both appearance and behavior.

While no single garment or article of clothing will make you blend in seamlessly into a crowd, certain clothing styles aid your attempts at blending in or, at least, obscure your identity. In the photo below, you probably noticed the person in the cap, despite the fact he is not in the foreground. Of the four people wearing hats in the photo, he was easiest to spot. First, the cap is red, and the bright color makes it stand out all by itself. The person in the foreground has on a hat that makes it unique to the other two solid-colored hats. Do you see the others wearing hats?

In colder seasons, reversible stocking caps do this with relative ease, especially if the colors are neutral colors and lack identifiable or recallable features. During warmer months, ball caps with the same parameters of neutral colors and no attention-grabbing features work equally well. The added benefit of the brim on a ball cap can help block surveillance cameras from capturing full images containing all of your facial features.

Smart apparel choices are necessary to incorporate the gray-man concept effectively. Photo courtesy of www.pixabay.com

Currently, there is a company manufacturing a ball cap called the Justice Cap that emits a signal that disrupts surveillance cameras. When an individual passes by a security camera, the device activates, disrupts the imaging so the wearer's face appears only as a white, indiscernible flash. I have yet to use one, but the concept is very intriguing and its uses countless.

The trendy, camouflage "operator" hats are great gun range hats, but they scream all sorts of warning indicators to others. Camouflage patterns like Multicam, A-TACS, and Kryptek are popular for these hats, but they can attract unwanted attention from people who are cognizant of the potential character, tactical ability, or prowess of its wearer. These hats overtly signal truths or assumptions such as, "I like, own, and shoot firearms", "I am a veteran, active military, or supporter of the military and gun rights", and "I practice or promote the concept of situational awareness". The patches displayed on the hats imply support or solidarity towards the subject, concepts or ideologies expressed on the patches. While I don't discourage the wearing of such hats, it is obvious that in certain areas, it would be unwise to draw the unnecessary attention to yourself.

I have the good fortune to have a low/no maintenance hairstyle. Should I choose to do so, I could wear one or two different wigs, drastically changing my appearance. On the opposite side of fortune, I have very poor vision that requires corrective lenses. This makes wearing off-the-rack sunglasses nearly impossible, unless I choose to look like a senior citizen driving a vehicle with the huge, "fit-over-your-glasses" sunglasses.

Pants are also paramount to blending in and not attracting attention to oneself. In American society, blue jeans are the most commonly accepted. Depending on where you come from and where you are, the denim color, cut, and fit of the jean may also be a factor to blending in. Despite the huge temptation, tactical pants--such as those manufactured by brands like Propper, 5.11 Tactical, Tru-Spec--should be avoided in large urban populations. Most unaware and blissfully ignorant civilians may not pay much heed to the clothes you wear. However, these types of pants make people stick out, especially among veterans, military contractors, and law enforcement personnel.

Camouflage patterns only compound the issue. Even the tactically neutral colors like khaki, coyote brown, olive drab, and even black can shift someone's focus onto you. If the color does not grab an observer's attention, it is usually the multiple utility pockets that alert him. An effective compromise can be reached with brands such as Carhartt, Dickie's, and Caterpillar. These brands are recognizable as well but do not draw the same scrutiny as the tactically recognized brands.

The main purpose of all clothing, of course, is to cover ourselves for protection, whether it from the elements or some other environmental factor. As long as it does not violate climate parameters, full-length pants and long sleeved shirts are usually acceptable and appropriate attire. Be certain to wear articles of clothing that cover identifiable birthmarks, scars, and tattoos.

Tattoos are always a key feature for law enforcement when searching and identifying suspects, especially gang tattoos. Tattoos, by design, are supposed to make the wearer stand out as an individual. About the only time you could truly get lost among a large crowd is at a tattoo convention. The same goes for piercings, whether it is the lips, eyebrows, ears, nose, or whatever, do yourself a favor and ditch the piercing. Not only will they make you more noticeable, but also in a street fight or in any other type of conflict, they are likely to become target points that produce large amounts of pain and possibly blood when grabbed, yanked, or twisted.

One of the most effective tactics one can use is the implementation of reversible gear and clothing. The more reversible articles of clothing you can have, the easier it is to thwart pursuers and still have some semblance of anonymity.

While I do not personally condone this practice, the "gangster lean" may have some legitimately plausible urban concealment advantages. This practice is seen frequently in urban districts and glamorized in rap songs, usually to promote the practices of pimping, drug dealing, and/or showing off personal possessions. The driver of a vehicle leans inward (right) or outward (left). By sheer coincidence, it makes judging an individual's height difficult.

The other closely related technique is reclining the driver seat back so that the headrest is even with the center pillar separating the driver's door and the rear passenger door. This prevents other vehicles overtaking from the left to view the driver's face until they have passed the hood of the car, forcing the occupants of the overtaking car to purposely turn and look.

The center pillar, because of its structural design is one of the stronger skeletal components of the vehicle. It is wide enough to obscure casual attempts to identify drivers and has the potential of stopping some small arms fire. This reclining method tends to be the widely accepted practice, especially in cities where gang violence is predominant. The downside is that it also reduces the driver's peripheral vision. If properly executed, this technique may aid in preventing positive identification at tollbooths, or some other loose checkpoint where a complete vehicle stop is not likely.

Vehicular concealment in an urban setting is problematic at best. Dull, drab military-inspired colors in a city is going to stick out (or at least appear drastically different) than the majority of glossy, metallic finishes. The best way is to have the most non-descript vehicle as possible, preferably in black, dark blue, silver, or white.

Over recent years, personal vehicles have become the epitome of moving billboards for the owners' personal information. I highly frown upon this practice. Everybody seems to want to let everyone else know what *their* rights are. Gun rights, religious rights, gay rights, favorite sports teams, political party affiliations, and the latest "support our cause" campaigns stickers plaster both windows and bumpers.

The 2016 presidential election is a prime example of people being targeted or identified by their political party affiliation and candidate of choice. Many supporters of Donald Trump reported cases of vandalism across the country, ranging from stolen yard signs to vehicles being keyed and tires slashed. Many of the victims voluntarily provided target indicators, not knowing or expecting to be targeted.

Some people go as far as telling you their family dynamics with themed stick figure family decals. Vanity license plates, their associated frames, objects hanging from the rearview mirror, and other custom additions all give clues about the owner. Parking permits and passes give clues to places of employment or the vicinity of where someone frequents.

One does not need to have a psychology degree, clairvoyance, or CIA training to work up a profile on someone who readily provides information to those who wish to take advantage of the free advertisement of such.

Study

Effective camouflage and concealment efforts require *subject* knowledge, *strategy*, *self-discipline*, and improving *skill-sets*.

Lastly, the most important S word to apply to your fieldcraft and camouflage/concealment skill-sets is *study*. Let your curiosity about your surroundings be the motivation to find out everything you possibly can about local plants and animals, terrain, climate, and other factors. The more you know, the more prepared you become, and the probability of your success greatly increases.

The study should systematically progress into practice. No one is a born expert when it comes to camouflage and concealment. Try to chart your progress, with the following example data log towards the end of this chapter. This will show you your strengths and bring your attention to areas needing improvement.

To maximize your study efforts, here are a few tools that will aid in your progress. With the invention of the smart phone, you really have the world at your fingertips, provided you have service in the area where you are scouting. The camera feature is indispensible for capturing land features, colors and textures, and can aid in the identification of vegetation growing in the area. Android Smartphone apps (e.g. Color Grab) and Color ID for Apple users, identify colors using the RGB and HEX codes for reproducing the colors you find during your area recon.

A good portion of your time studying is firmly rooted in the practices of scouting and reconnaissance. Your attention to the various types of surroundings and the living and nonliving things that exist within that particular environment will greatly contribute to your concealment success. It does take a certain amount of strategy to study carefully the numerous amounts of plant and tree life potentially found in any given area.

While it may not be necessary to become a botanist with a Bachelor's or Master's Degree, simply studying the native vegetation in your environment will aid in choosing the required colors and textures to replicate effectively the existing vegetation.

Likewise, in your study, you may discover a plant type that has a reasonable facsimile to a commercially available artificial plant. Go to your local arts and crafts store and walk through the aisles of artificial greenery and foliage and you'll be amazed at what you can pass off as natural-looking vegetation. The nice thing about artificial vegetation is it does not wilt and brown out the way natural vegetation does when cut and applied to ghillie suits.

As your skills progress, you should try to collaborate with other like-minded individuals to have them actively search for you. It is one thing to hide when no one is looking for you, but your own senses become heightened and the adrenaline rush produced help you to experience and understand the physiological sensations when others are actively and purposely searching for you.

Fieldcraft is the key ingredient to all camouflage and concealment endeavors. You can wear the best camouflage pattern available or even a ghillie suit, but if you go casually traipsing through the woods, animals and people will know you are there. There are additional resources in the resources section at the end of the book for those who wish a more extensive discussion on tracking and counter-tracking techniques.

Counter-Tracking and K-9 Evasion Techniques

This next portion may seem controversial as it pertains to the deliberate evasion of personnel and K-9 units from a strict, SERE (Survival, Evasion, Resistance, and Escape) standpoint. In no way do I advocate or condone intentional law-breaking or resisting arrest, fleeing with the intent to evade police, or assaulting/attacking police officers while they are acting according to the lawfully prescribed and accepted methods of modern policing.

With that being stated, it may be necessary to evade guard dogs used by drug cartels, enemy patrols, wartime trackers, or a pursuant(s) for unique survival scenarios. While I hope that readers will never find themselves in this type of circumstance, the information is provided, nevertheless. So again, I will echo my disclaimer that I do not condone the use of this information to commit illegal activities.

Contrary to the portrayals in action films, some of the tactics used to thwart a canine's keen sense of smell is about as successful as trying to flick off individual grains of black pepper off a pile of dirt while wearing handcuffs and boxing gloves. A canine's sense of smell is so much more developed than humans, that saying a canine's sense of smell is a million times stronger than ours is almost not an exaggeration. While all dogs have a keen sense of smell, only specific dog breeds, such as bloodhounds, are truly effective man trackers.

I once read an online article on fieldcraft written by David Reed where he suggested various liquid or powder irritants in certain portions of your path would not cover up your scent, but it might impair the canine's nose.[1] Hunter's Specialties makes a product called Windicator. It is a small plastic squeeze bottle filled with talcum powder designed to help determine wind direction and speed for the purpose of scent dispersion while hunting. A similar bottle filled with cayenne pepper or other nasal irritant would fit easily in a pocket or pack.

I have heard of people attempting to use cocaine, but I wonder why someone would choose to possess a controlled substance. During World War II, blood was mixed with cocaine to throw off German K-9 units.[1] Cocaine and other controlled substances aside, I am of the opinion that most attempts to remove or manipulate the scent trail are risky, at best. Nevertheless, I list some of them for their entertainment value and creativity. There is no 100-percent certainty guaranteed with any of the listed techniques, but if an opportunity presents itself, some of these may work against certain breeds and lesser-trained K-9 teams.

A trip-wire with a canister of oleoresin capsicum (OC) spray positioned at knee level may also sideline the K-9 unit for a while, but the downside is this confirms to the pursuit teams that they are still on the right track, unless used in conjunction with another deception technique to throw pursuers off the trail. Trip-wires are never a sure bet, so spraying pepper spray on the bottom of your shoes may prove more successful in discouraging a canine from zeroing in on your scent.

One of the more deceptive techniques is using porcupine quills. This involves carrying a substantial amount of porcupine quills and standing them upright upon the path you are leaving. Space the quills no more than 1 inch apart and loosely cover them, deliberately leaving some scent. Porcupine quills and the thorns from Hawthorn trees, also called May trees (*Crataegus Monogyna*) appear much more natural than manufactured caltrops. This potentially can do a couple of things.

First, the canine may step on the thorns or quills, embedding into the pads of the foot, immediately stopping the K-9 unit to address the injury and administer first aid. Second, if the scent is strong enough and the quills concealed enough, the canine may put its nose directly into the quills, again producing injury to the nose. If either of the two scenarios produces consecutively successful results, the canine may associate your scent with pain and may grow reluctant to stay on the trail. The handler might not assume a deliberate attack on the canine until the second or third time, or maybe not at all. With the exception of the extreme Southern states and the Great Plains states, either porcupine quills, hawthorn tree thorns, or both can be found.

Reasonable debate exists as to whether the life of a trained police canine is, or should be considered to be on the same level as that of a uniformed officer in a value of life context. My opinion is simple. I have owned pets and rescued animals from potential harm, but I believe the canine does not have a soul or the intellectual capacity to understand the concepts of morality, the force continuum, and officer discretion. It solely acts and responds to the commands of its handler.

While the loss of a canine in the line of duty is emotionally heartbreaking due to the bond between the canine and handler, and creates a financial loss to the departmental agency, I do not consider the canine to be on the same level of mortal existence as human life--as unpopular as this notion may be. My opinion is the same even if the canine is the property of a law enforcement agency. In a bona fide SERE-type scenario, I believe that human life trumps the lives of animals, regardless of the intrinsic value placed on them by humans. Therefore, if necessary and possible in a SERE scenario, eliminate the canine.

Determining the weakest link in any K-9 unit is sometimes difficult and may be a crapshoot. Any successful chance of evading a K-9 team focuses on wearing out or confusing the handler or the canine. These attempts should set your primary attention on one or the other. Confusing both the handler and the canine alternately sometimes allows one to regroup and rest. It is a good strategy to be in much better physical condition than the human component of any K-9 team. Canines have great stamina and endurance, so wearing out the dog can be an exercise in futility. Here are five suggested tips I have found to help avoid K-9 search units:

- Early Detection - know or assume that others are pursuing you.
- Navigate through high population areas/ environments.
- Watch your step when traveling through wooded areas.
- Urinate on different trees/objects in a triangular pattern.
- Understand canine weaknesses - Canines are restrained by their owner
- Carry an OC/pepper spray.[2]

Police and military canines are formidable adversaries when faced with SERE scenarios, but most breeds are susceptible to good counter-tracking practices. Photo courtesy of www.pixabay.com

Despite all these efforts, eliminating your scent to the point of being undetectable is impossible for a highly trained, man-tracking K-9 unit. You can wash your clothing in unscented soaps formulated for hunters, wear scent-blocking clothing, and use cover scents and still be detected and tracked. Despite all of the available options, the best course of action is to ambush and take out the K-9 unit. This is only advisable if your life is in absolute, eminent peril. It should be noted that special operations groups avoid K-9 units at all costs because of the K-9's ability to compromise the mission. If contact is unavoidable with a K-9 unit, it usually ends with a dirt nap for both the hound and handler.

Another vital piece of information to study when dealing with potential K-9 threats is the common commands used by handlers to instruct the dog's actions. Typically, most police and military working dogs receive instruction in a foreign language. Doing this primarily keeps the dog on task despite the verbal attempts of a suspect or adversary to call off or stop the dog from performing its instructed duties.

For years, German was the most common foreign language used, but now other European languages such as French, Czech, Polish, Dutch, and even Hungarian are used. Dr. Mark Plonsky, (aka Dr. P) a Professor of Psychology at the University of Wisconsin-Stevens Point is also an experimental biopsychologist with expertise in animal learning and behavior.[3] His website, and several other websites dedicated to K-9 working dog training, list the common canine commands in the aforementioned foreign languages to help handlers learn verbal commands and their pronunciation. I am very fortunate to have married a woman who speaks fluent German. Foreign language skills are boundless in their real world applications. This is yet another example of the benefits of learning a foreign language.

The stress involved in a trained K-9 attack is very high, and the ability to recall the appropriate verbal command to stop the assault needs to be developed and maintained. The more you memorize and practice the commands, the more confidence you will have. You may even consider using them for your own guard dog. With this said, this is not a guarantee to stop a K-9 attack. Some, if not all, of military and police K-9 units are so well trained that only the voice of their handler will cease the canine's actions.

Tracking and Tactical Movement Tips

Note: *Although this section could justifiably appear in the chapter on shifting, the following tactical movement points and table give practical advice regarding shifting strategies and skill-set acquisition. The self-discipline and student initiative required to learn the skills is the reason why they are listed here in the study chapter.*

Among the most fundamental requirements for tactical movement is practice and realistic, skill-focused training. Scores of fieldcraft books and military manuals dedicated to the topic go beyond the scope of this work. However, I feel it important enough to include some basic tips that directly correlate to camouflage and concealment discipline. I have found the bullet-type format is helpful for memorization and quick-reference.[4]

- Never move in a straight line.
- Move in general directions towards objectives.
- Move at night. Darkness is one of your best advantages.

- Consider all trails, streams and open areas as potential dangers.
- Avoid bending/breaking branches off trees, bushes, and shrubs.
- Use the native sounds and weather to conceal movements.
- Never move quickly, especially when startled.
- Avoid using trails at all costs.
- Carefully cross streams to avoid knocking debris into the water or stirring up silt and mud.
- Do not use small trees or saplings to climb up inclines or to balance yourself.
- Carry a good quality, nonreflective field knife.[4]

Another good stalking and movement strategy are the techniques employed by snipers, hunters, and trackers. While walking upright is the fastest, it is also the most visually compromising method. At the other end of the spectrum, the worm crawl is a time-consuming, energy-expending exercise in patience and endurance. A good way to practice your low or worm crawl is to stalk turkeys. Turkeys have excellent vision and hearing and are very difficult to sneak up on undetected.

Practice Makes Perfect

There is only one effective way to learn how to move with greater stealth and that is to practice. The great thing about this fieldcraft skill is you can practice it anywhere you walk. You may not want to attract unnecessary attention with the short-stridden gait of the fox walk in crowded or highly public areas, but you could practice in the line at the grocery store or any place where standing in a line is customary or expected. Focus on the sound of your walk and practice walking on a variety of different materials, from dried leaves to pea gravel, reducing the sound of your footfalls as you do so.

Movement	Profile	Speed	Maneuverability	Visual Detection
Fox Walk	Very High	Very High	Very High	Very High
Crouch	High	High	High	High
High Crawl	Medium	Medium	Medium	Medium
Low Crawl	Low	Low	Low	Low
Worm Crawl	Very Low	Very Low	Very Low	Very Low

Tactical Movement Chart[5]

On the opposite end of the shifting spectrum is the static aspect of concealment. This requires you to practice sitting as motionless as possible for long periods. Learn to sit or lie in awkward, uncomfortable positions, as you may not always have the luxury of acceptable or regarded as "comfortable" static accommodations. The table on the next page is an example of a worksheet designed to help you practice and record your camouflage and concealment skills. Use it to practice your concealment skill sets.

To a certain degree, this activity has plenty of benefits. In addition to the calming effects of being close to nature, you gain valuable experience prior to your favorite hunting season. Remaining motionless and quiet allows all of the surrounding nature to "normalize" back to its previous state before your arrival. So often humans are the invaders, and all sorts of wildlife will scamper off or chirp to alert your presence to the other wildlife in the area. For this reason, it is a good practice to listen and recognize the various sounds of birds and animals used to alert the other species of your intrusion.

CAMOUFLAGE & CONCEALMENT WORKSHEET

Date:	Location:							Temperature:		Wind:
Camouflage Pattern:			Season: S S A W	Conditions:						
DETECTOR:		DISTANCE:	CONCEALMENT:		COVER:		DETECTION:		CAUSE:	
Human	Animal	Yards/Meters	Partial Camo	Full Camo	Partial	Exposed	Active	Incidental	Reason Code*	
1										
2										
3										
4										
5										
6										
7										
8										
9										
10										
11										
12										
13										
14										
15										

*Reason Codes: **V**- Visual (Non-Motion), **M** - Movement, **S** - Sound, **O**- Odor   © 2016 Hidden Success Tactical

A larger, downloadable version is also available at the Hidden Success Tactical website, www.hiddensuccesstactical.com

Learning how to sit still and be quiet can be a challenging task, but is necessary for camouflage and concealment success. Make a copy of the "Camouflage & Concealment Worksheet" above or download it from the Hidden Success Tactical website for free, and use it to help you track and record your practice. Review the data card with the other participants so they can help you determine the hows and whys of their detection of you. It is really a more purpose-driven game of hide-n-seek.

I remember one personal hunting story my father told of a rather unsuspecting chipmunk that ran the length of my father's rifle barrel during a black bear hunt in Ontario, Canada. It hopped on the muzzle end of the barrel and walked the gauntlet until it reached the receiver. The chipmunk perched himself on the rifle breach and engaged him in a 10-second staring contest before he shooed it off.

This is an example of an excellent training photo. The object of interest is far enough away, not centered, and not overly concealed behind cover. Can you see where the person is hiding? Photo credit: GhillieSuits.com, Inc/Todd Muirhead

I have had deer and wild hogs come within ten yards or less of my position, just by being quiet and still. With favorable wind and remaining upwind, I have heard of several hunters who have physically touched their prey with their rifle or shotgun barrels. There are countless videos on the internet that show up-close-and-personal wildlife encounters. You will be amazed at what you can see and hear when you remain quiet and still.

Another important way to improve your camouflage and concealment skills is to take or have someone else take photographs while hiding. However, when doing this, make sure to avoid the common mistake of centering the object (you) in the center of the photographs. You become too easy to find, even when you cannot see all the details. This is the major downfall with most photographs found on the internet featuring ghillie suits. With that said, most people center objects in a pictures and photographs for focal point reasons. Manufacturers do this so they can show the product in as close to "real-world" conditions as they can without confusing or irritating the potential customer, who does not want to needlessly search for products.

When taking these training photos, you should not hide completely or overuse existing cover because the objective is to be able to evaluate your skills through these photographs. Of course, in real-life scenarios, you should use whatever cover you have in order to hide effectively.

To show all the S words together, I created a modified infographic on page 98 containing all of the S words of camouflage and concealment in this book. It puts them into context and shows all the related inter-dependencies that make camouflage effective. Attention to detail is one of the best teachers. See how long it takes to spot the duplicated word.

Let us also not forget the several C's of Camouflage. There is no need for an exercise in expository redundancy. However, a further study of the following words and their relationship to the aforementioned concepts will enhance your knowledge and understanding on the subject.

Crypsis
Conditions
Cover
Climate

Color
Cluster
Clues
Covert
Cloaking
Contrast
Content
Concealment

For one more final kick to the proverbial dead horse, the following list features the D's of Camouflage and their relationship to the world of camouflage.

Disguise
Disruption
Design
Dispersion
Dissipation
Duality
Discipline
Detection
Details
Distance
Direction
Decay
Deception
Distraction
Data

Conclusion

With the information presented in this book, along with the application and practice of its methods, you too will *appear to vanish*!

The S's of Effective Camouflage and Concealment

Resources for Supplies and Additional Instruction

Websites:
www.ghilliesuits.com
www.hiddensuccesstactical.com
www.itstactical.com
www.justicecaps.com
www.naturereliance.org
www.practicalprimitive.com
www.scottdonelantrackingschool.com
www.snakebitetactical.com
www.survivalschool.us
www.tacticalconcealment.com
www.tacticaltrackertraining.com
www.tycunningham.org
www.willowhavenoutdoor.com

Related Books:
ACM IV Security Services - *Surveillance Countermeasures*, Paladin Press, 1994, 2005
Ahearn, Frank M. with Horan, Eileen C. - *How to Disappear*, Globe Pequot Press, 2010
Carss, Bob - *The SAS Guide to Tracking*, First Lyons Press, 2009

Dermody, Matthew - *Hidden Success: A Comprehensive Guide to Ghillie Suit Construction*, 2012

Forbes, Tom - *The Invisible Advantage Workbook*, Paladin Press, 2002

Hartcup, Guy - *Camouflage: The History of Concealment & Deception in War*, Pen & Sword Military, 2008

Luna, J.J. - *How to Be Invisible*, St. Martin's Press, 2012

Plaster, Major John L. USAR (ret.) - *The Ultimate Sniper: An advanced training manual for military and police snipers*, Paladin Press, 2006

Ritch, Van - *Rural Surveillance: A Cops Guide to Gathering Evidence in Remote Areas*, Paladin Press, 2003

Scott-Donelan, David - *Tactical Tracking Operations: The Essential Guide to Military and Police Trackers*, Paladin Press, 1998

Starnater, Eddie - *Principles of Natural Camouflage: The Art of Invisibility*, CreateSpace Independent Publishing Platform, 2015

Recommended Online Articles:

Techniques for Countering Thermal Imaging Devices - http://mail.blockyourid.com/~gbpprorg/mil/thermal/index.html

Why American Civilians Need a Thermal Evasion Suits, Smith, Brandon, http://www.snakebitetactical.com/essays.html

Making Thermal Evasion Possible, Smith, Brandon, http://www.snakebitetactical.com/essays.html

References

Chapter 1:

[1]*Webster's New World Dictionary, Third College Ed.* 1991,
[2] http://www.slideshare.net/IF109/camouflage-for-the-patriot -   slide 2 of 87
[3]Brad Turner, 2005, 2008
[4]United States Army, *Camouflage FM 5-20*, May 1968
[5]ITS Tactical Crew, *Target Detection and Identification*, July 19, 2010,
[6]Starnater, Eddie - *Principles of Natural Camouflage: The Art of Invisibility*, CreateSpace Independent Publishing Platform, 2015, pg. 53
[7]http://www.willowhavenoutdoor.com, *How to Disappear in the Wilderness: A Natural Camouflage Tutorial*, June 2, 2014
[8]Starnater, Eddie - *Principles of Natural Camouflage: The Art of Invisibility*, CreateSpace Independent Publishing Platform, 2015, pg. 23

Chapter 2:

[1]Brad Turner, www.roggenwolf.com website 2005, 2008
[2]von Besser, Kurt- *How Games Animals See and Smell*, ATSKO/SNO-SEAL, Inc. 2002,
[3]Quote from Arnold Schwarzenegger's character in James Cameron's 1984 science fiction movie, *The Terminator*.

Chapter 3:

[1]Brad Turner, www.roggenwolf.com website 2005, 2008
[2]Brad Turner, www.roggenwolf.com website 2005, 2008
[3] Brad Turner, www.roggenwolf.com website 2005, 2008
[4]https://en.wikipedia.org/wiki/Chromophore

Chapter 4:
[1]Plaster, Major John L., USAR (Ret.), *Advanced Ultimate Sniper DVD,* Paladin Press, 1997
[2]Plaster, Major John L., USAR (Ret.), *Ultimate Sniper: An advanced training manual for military and police snipers,* Paladin Press, Boulder, CO, 1993, 2006, pg. 374

Chapter 5:
[1]http://www.ces.fau.edu/nasa/module-2/radiation-sun.php,
[2]*Using Color Infrared (CIR) Imagery: A Guide for Understanding, Interpreting and Benefiting from CIR Imagery,* Prepared for the North Carolina Geographic Information Coordinating Council by the Statewide Mapping Advisory Committee, Working Group for Orthophotography Planning, July 2011, pg. 2-4
[3]https://www.oathkeepers.org/defeating-drones-how-to-build-a-thermal-evasion-suit/ www.snakebitetactical.com
[4]Starnater, Eddie - *Principles of Natural Camouflage: The Art of Invisibility,* CreateSpace Independent Publishing Platform, 2015, pg. 20
[5]Cramer, Guy - *U.S. Army Phase IV Baseline Patterns, will the Army have to settle with these? Part 6,* http://www.hyperstealth.com/baseline/

Chapter 6:
[1]https://www.youtube.com/watch?v=hjnhnmBU_rU

Chapter 7: none

Chapter 8:
[1]Walker, Brad - <u>Cabela's ColorPhase Changes the Hunt, Will it Change the Battlefield?</u> Aug. 9, 2013,

http://kitup.military.com/2013/08/cabelas-colorphase-game-change.html

[2]Dermody, Matthew, *Hidden Success: A Comprehensive Guide to Ghillie Suit Construction*, Self-published, 2012
[3]Plaster, Major John L., USAR (Ret.), *Advanced Ultimate Sniper DVD,* Paladin Press, 1997
[4]Dermody, Matthew, *Hidden Success*, 2012
[5]Dermody, Matthew, *Hidden Success*, 2012
[6]Dermody, Matthew, *Hidden Success*, 2012
[7]Dermody, Matthew, *Hidden Success*, 2012
[8]Ibid.

Chapter 9
[1]www.tacrescue.com/blending-in-the-grey-man-concept/

Chapter 10:
[1]https://graftedinelena.wordpress.com/2013/01/24/rabbits-blood-and-cocaine/
[2]www.theprepperproject.com/how-to-evade-search-dogs/
[3] http://www4.uwsp.edu/psych/dog/info.htm
[4]Ritch, Van, *Rural Surveillance: A cop's guide to Gathering Evidence in Remote Areas*, Paladin Press, 2003, pgs 72-75
[5]Chart adaptation based upon information found at https://www.youtube.com/watch?v=Sv_2T4Q_y-I

About the Author

   Matthew Dermody is an author of three books on the subject of camouflage and concealment, as well as writing guest blogs and articles featured on survival websites. He maintains his own website focusing on the educational and instructional aspects of the art of camouflage. He is available for consultation and offers training seminars for both law enforcement/military personnel and civilians. He currently lives in the Inland Northwest region of the United States with his wife and twin daughters.

You may visit his website: www.hiddensuccesstactical.com and follow him on Facebook, Instagram, and Twitter.

Facebook: Hidden Success Tactical
Instagram: Hidden Success Tactical
Twitter: @AppearToVanish

Made in the USA
San Bernardino, CA
30 April 2020